MENTAL TOUGHNESS AND CHANGE YOUR LIFE

IMPROVE HEALTHY HABITS TO ACHIEVE SUCCESS AND HAPPY RELATIONSHIPS. SELF HELP FOR POSITIVE THINKING. EMPATH'S SURVIVAL GUIDE AND SELF DEVELOPMENT

David Robert Jones

© **Copyright 2020 - All rights reserved.**

The content contained within this book may not be reproduced, duplicated or transmitted without direct written permission from the author or the publisher.

Under no circumstances will any blame or legal responsibility be held against the publisher, or author, for any damages, reparation, or monetary loss due to the information contained within this book. Either directly or indirectly.

Legal Notice:

This book is copyright protected. This book is only for personal use. You cannot amend, distribute, sell, use, quote or paraphrase any part, or the content within this book, without the consent of the author or publisher.

Disclaimer Notice:

Please note the information contained within this document is for educational and entertainment purposes only. All effort has been executed to present accurate, up to date, and reliable, complete information. No warranties of any kind are declared or implied. Readers acknowledge that the author is not engaging in the rendering of legal, financial, medical or professional advice. The content within this book has been derived from various sources. Please consult a licensed professional before attempting any techniques outlined in this book.

By reading this document, the reader agrees that under no circumstances is the author responsible for any losses, direct or indirect, which are incurred as a result of the use of information contained within this document, including, but not limited to, — errors, omissions, or inaccuracies.

Table of Contents

Introduction 6

Chapter 1 Begin Changing Your Habits 10

Chapter 2 Habit For Personal Development 18

Chapter 3 Positive Thinking: Big Scam, Miracle Solution, Or Real Tool? ... 26

Chapter 4 Enjoy Your Empathy 36

Chapter 5 Mental Toughness - High Frustration Tolerance 44

Chapter 6 Habits, Rituals & Daily Practices 52

Chapter 7 Feeling Your Feelings 60

Chapter 8 How To Stop Absorbing Negative Energies. 70

Chapter 9 How To Make Good Achievement Driven Habits 76

Chapter 10 Analyze The Way You Think And Look The World 84

Chapter 11 The Relationship Between Overthinking, Anxiety, Stress, And Negative Thinking 92

Chapter 12 How To Manage Your Time Efficiently? 100

Chapter 13 Start, Do, Achieve 108

Chapter 14 Coping With Depression 116

Chapter 15 The Tools You Need 124

Chapter 16 Realigning Your Confidence Levels With Your Abilities 132

Chapter 17 Improve Your Attitude 142

Chapter 18 The Purpose Of Your Life 150

Conclusion 160

Introduction

Do you believe that everything happens for a reason? I do. I believe that what you need will always find its way to you. Something is missing in your life, something that your soul is longing for. Something bigger and wildly abundant that is waiting for you right around the corner. The only thing standing between you and whatever that "something" is, is you, or more specifically, your mindset.

This is going to help you identify and transform the limiting beliefs that are blocking you from all the abundant possibilities that await you, so that you can get serious about what you want and take action toward making it happen. Do not worry; I am going to give you the tools you need to do it all with ease.

I'm excited and honored to travel along on this journey with you. My greatest wish is that the information in this is as transformational for you as it has been for me, and the many people I've had the privilege of sharing it with.

You might be wondering what kind of impact this will make in your life. All I can say is this: Just try it! Give it a good, honest, and consistent effort. Once you start to feel a shift in your energy, you'll get to witness your desires begin to manifest right before your eyes and start to see what can only be described as miracles happening everywhere.

I wasn't always a believer. I was a big-time skeptic of mindset work at first. It all sounded a little too "woo" to me. So, if you're in the same camp, wondering if this is going to work for you, this is a perfect introduction, as there is a healthy balance of practicality throughout. I promise not to go too woo on you!

If, however, you've been on the mindset bandwagon for a while, this is going to help you take your practice to the next level and beyond. That's because I take everything you already know about a positive mindset and the Laws of Attraction and Vibration and put it into a repeatable system you can implement again and again to get the results you want.

Whether you're a mindset newbie or a seasoned vet, you'll find a tremendous amount of value in this, and I look forward to helping you ditch your limits and take control of the life you've been dreaming about and deserve.

While your vision board can be a huge source of inspiration and motivation, it can also be a compass of sorts. Sometimes, it can be all too easy to get so caught up in the motions of pursuing a goal that you lose track of the destination itself. This can result in you making less progress than you imagine, or even worse, making some choices along the way that serve to take you further away from your goal rather than closer to it. By constantly reminding yourself of where it is you are trying to get, you can better judge whether or not you are going in the right direction.

Another way that your vision board can help keep you going in the right direction is by showing you the changes you need for success.

Sometimes, you might find that you have a behavior or a mindset that undermines your efforts, thereby standing between you and the success you desire. Whenever you identify such an obstacle, you can put something on your vision board to encourage you to overcome it. Any inspirational quotes or motivational writings that address the things you are trying to overcome will give you the strength you need to make those necessary changes in your life.

Cheers to a mind-blowing journey.

Chapter 1 Begin Changing Your Habits

It is time now to begin looking at the issues you have with some of your habits in the face and to replace them with more enriching, and greatly positive ones. Do your best to remain judgment-free while you are doing this, and to forgive yourself for any minor setbacks. Before you begin trying to change certain habits, it may be best to try to assess what level of change you are at.

This is another point where access to your note would be helpful.

The Stages of Change

Look over the list you made of habits you want to instill in your life.

Now, we are going to go through what is called the Stages of Change: The Transtheoretical Model was written in the 1970s by psychologists who were observing people who were trying to quit smoking. They wanted to record the various stages in which they all traveled through that would eventually lead them to take a proactive approach in their healthcare.

The stages are listed as follows:

1. Pre-contemplation: People in this stage don't plan to take action in the foreseeable future, which is defined as within at least six months. People here are usually not aware that their behavior isn't good for them or others. They are not aware of the many pros that exist should they decide to change their behavior.

2. Contemplation: People in this stage begin intended to start down the healthy path in the foreseeable future, at least the next six months. People may not see that their behavior is problematic, and are more thoughtful about the pros that are involved with their decisions to make a change.

3. Preparation: People are ready in this stage to take action within the next 30 days. People begin taking small steps forward, and believe that this change will help them to live a healthier life.

4. Action: Within this stage, people have taken action to change their behavior and intend to keep moving forward with this change.

5. Maintenance: At this stage, people have been able to sustain their behavior change for at least six months now, and intend to maintain this behavior going forward in their lives. People in this stage also work to prevent relapsing back into old, unhealthy behaviors.

6. Termination: Within this final stage, people have no desire to return to their unhealthy behavior, and are confident that they are not going to relapse. (This stage is rarely reached as it is very definite; it is usually only used when describing health problems and their changes).

Actual Neural Rewiring

The use of the word 'rewiring' in this title wasn't written for the show. The science of neurology, which is the study of the brain and how it affects human thought and behavior, has proven that there are various ways that humans can reshape the flow of neurons moving through their spine and brain. It was once thought that every person's brain is wired a certain way, and very little can be done about it throughout their lives. Thankfully, through the application of new behaviors and experiences, this is not a fact and something you have vast control over.

Neuroplasticity refers to your brain's ability to reorganize, both physically and functionally, throughout your entire life with influences from the environment, your behavior, thinking, and emotions. Neural pruning refers to the natural process of the brain to extinguish any neuron that isn't being fired. You strengthen certain neural pathways, the more you engage in the same thought patterns, behavior, emotions, interactions, etc. This is essentially how learning a new skill works; you start one way, and if you participate in this hobby consistently, the neural pathway that is associated with it will become stronger, warmer, and more instantly activated.

This process is the key to understanding how instilling new habits work. There is a reason why when you tried to stretch your injured muscles only three times last week, then forgot one week, and then only did it twice another, that this behavior did not become a habit. The neural pathway simply wasn't warm enough, and neurons are only going to fire when they are being summoned often.

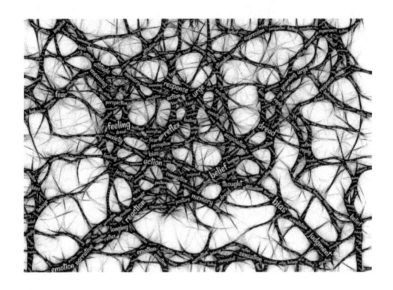

Steps to Take to Begin Creating New Habits

The following is a template that you can apply to any of the habits that you want to create for yourself, along with the ones you want to get rid of.

1. Identify Cues: There is something that has to trigger a habit, and a cue can be anything that relates to it; maybe stress makes you want food, alcohol, or a certain thought or post on social media makes you want to procrastinate. Whatever it may be, try to notice these. If this is hard for you to do, try to notice when you are engaging in a bad habit, and then going back from there. Did someone say something to you? Did you read something on the internet? Are you worried about something? Do you best to honestly reflect yourself?

2. Disrupt: Once you have noticed the cues that are triggering your chosen bad habit, you can begin trying to throw it off. For example, if reading something on social media makes you feel bad about yourself and your skills, which makes you want to sit on the couch and procrastinate, try limiting your social media activity, or at least not doing it in the morning, or the time you feel most affected.

3. Replace: Research has shown that if you have a more positive habit in mind to replace a bad one, you are more likely to stop participating in the bad one. The new habit interferes with the old one, making it harder for your brain to go on autopilot, and go down the path with those warm neural pathways. A good example of this is trying to replace night-time snacks with fruit or something healthier; not having junk food available may also be another step-in disarming that bad eating habit.

4. Keep it Simple: Making new behaviors simply goes in line with the old behaviors; those were easy too, which is why you have engaged with them for so long. Making a new habit too difficult will make the application of it far less appealing.

5. Think Long Term: Habits generally form because they satisfy short-term impulses. Though, the results of these short-term impulses may last a while, such as avoiding cleaning the dishes or stretching your injured leg. When you are engaging in new habits, try to think about the long-term effects that this will have on your life and how you are doing it for the best for yourself.

6. Persist: Habits are hard to break; that's why there are so many writes about forming new ones! We order in at night because it is easy, and we don't want to make dinner. This may be because we had a long, tiring day at work, and we did not bring enough food for lunch and can't be bothered to rummage up a home-cooked meal. We also may have no brought the right amount of food for lunch because we did not plan the night before, staying up late and lying on the couch. This kind of habit connects to many other bad habits, so, if we look at this as an example, where to begin would be to start making lunches for the week that are substantial enough to feel full. Then, you will have more energy to cook a healthier, financially sound dinner.

Instilling a new habit is going to take time. While you are looking over your list of new behavioral habits to apply, take a glance at this next list, which will give you advice on how you can improve your mental strength while putting in the effort to make healthier, happier choices.

1. Create Behavioral Experiments to Challenge Your Self-Limiting Beliefs: There is probably more than one reason why you haven't been able to keep up with a certain habit in your life. You may suffer from mental health disorders, or even have become used to self-diminishing dialogue. Whatever it may be, it doesn't make you less capable than anyone else or mean that you possess less mental strength than other people. Your self-limiting beliefs are simply trying to convince you of these lies. So, you may need to change those first before you start looking at behavioral habits.

2. Replace Victim Language with Empowering Statements: Self-limiting beliefs are more than likely going to be made worse by the constant use of victim language. You may employ this within your self-dialogue on the daily. If you catch yourself blaming others for how you feel, or the negative circumstances in your life, stop yourself. This is the victim language. It makes you feel like you are not in control of your daily life. Try to replace it with statements that you feel like you ARE in control; because you are! You deserve to recognize that you are in the driver's seat of the life that you are living in.

3. Practice Self-Compassion: Calling yourself names and putting yourself down isn't going to motivate you to try again, or to try anything else that is challenging for the matter. If you want to do better, think about how you would talk to someone you love after they make a mistake or something negative happens in their lives. If you are a reasonable person, you wouldn't sit and insult them for hours on end. You would show them compassion, empathy, and support them in making new decisions about the future. Try to do this for yourself and recognize that this is only going to help you in the long run, as bringing yourself down is only going to make you feel unhealthy and unhappy.

4. Behave like the Person You Want to Become: Wishing that you could be a certain way isn't going to make it happen. Wishing that you could be a morning person or a person that exercises daily isn't going to do anything but make you feel bad for yourself. You are capable of becoming these things, and the first step toward that becoming is trying to act like that person. Ask yourself, what would a morning person too? And follow through on those answers.

5. Live in The Moment: This is going to be a repeated notion throughout this, as lack of living the moment is a consistent cause of unhappiness, lack of health, and various mental health disorders. Staying within the moment and getting what you can out of it is the only way that you can improve yourself and reach the future that you have been planning for.

Since there are many habits that people, in general, want to instill in these lives, this will explore some of the more common and pervasive habits that can help you're as a whole.

Chapter 2
Habit for Personal Development

Personal development is the process of maximizing your talents and potential, enhancing the quality of your life, and reaching your aspirations.

One of the benefits of personal development is that it helps you achieve self-awareness. So many people go about their lives without understanding themselves at a deeper level. But it is through personal development that a person gets to take a peek into what they are like as a person. Once you are self-aware, you acquire a great understanding of the things that trigger you, the things that you have a passion for, but most importantly, you get to understand your thoughts and feelings. Self-awareness is a skill that helps you make helpful decisions in life. So many people become consumed in the raging chaos of life, and they seem unaware of the precise actions to take to get where they hope to be. Personal development helps you recognize your potential and utilize your skills for maximum gain. There are so many people with amazing capabilities, but they are unable to utilize their potential because they are not even aware of what they are capable of achieving. Personal development involves challenging yourself and stepping out of your comfort zones. And this tendency helps you overcome your limitations, put your skills to great use, and develop a great tolerance against challenges and high-pressure situations.

Personal development also helps people to have a sense of direction. If you have not taken into personal development, you could be wandering around, looking for your way in the world, but only crashing into stumbling blocks. Nevertheless, when you take up personal development, you can now understand the precise direction you want your life to take. For instance, if you are an extremely gifted person, and seem to have an intelligent perception of life, it can cause you to have uncommon ideas and perspective of life. You can easily lose focus and allow the voices in your mind to mislead you. However, personal development would help you understand your capabilities and draft your plan for success. You get to understand your strengths and weaknesses and develop the right approach. No matter what you decide to do with your life, there'll always be opposition and challenges, but you must not let these challenges overwhelm you and make you stop trying. All successful people have a vision, and they never stop going towards it even when the challenges are many. Challenges should inspire you to attain excellence, not cower, and admit defeat.

Personal development also helps you to have focus and work toward your goals without letting distractions get in the way. Most people can hardly stay focused on a task because they have got a lot going inside their minds, and it keeps them from achieving their important life goals. Personal development helps an individual cultivate the skill of concentrating and never letting any distractions take away your focus. To scale the heights of success, you will always need to be hard-working. Thus, you will need to be focused. Personal development helps you understand yourself and come up with a plan that will see you sticking to your work and giving it your all. When it comes to achieving success, it is not enough to merely work, but be productive. You must ensure that you are engaged in something productive and achieving results. This is what elevates you to the next level.

Personal development also helps you become an effective person. In every field, many people are offering various services, and yet you would stick to one person because they have proved themselves effective. Personal development helps you learn how to be effective in your execution of work and achieve the best results.

Motivation is another benefit of personal development. You won't always be in a mood of applying yourself and achieving the results that you want. You won't always be in the mental frame of work. In such situations, it is easy to avoid working and indulge in some other distracting activities. But then, personal development helps us increase our motivation. The best kind of motivation stems from a genuine passion for an activity as opposed to the expectations of rewards. Thanks to personal development, you can look within yourself and realize what you are passionate about. Thus, you are guaranteed motivation. If you have no motivation, it can be pretty hard to achieve the kind of success that you have always yearned for, considering that you will put in less work. It doesn't matter how tough your assignment might appear objectively. Motivation helps you approach that task with a smile on your face. Motivated people never stop pushing back their limits. Once they achieve one goal, they immediately start aiming for the next goal, enabling them to create a lasting legacy.

Personal development also helps you develop resilience. The world is very competitive. You may think that your ideas are the best, but if you don't reinforce them, if you don't fight for them ceaselessly, you will end up defeated. Resilience is the ability to never accept defeat. Most people don't want to jump into the ring because they are scared of failing. But then, there's nothing wrong with failing as long as you stand up and fight again. Before you achieve a goal, you are going to have to go through failure. Don't let failure define your life, but rather take your lesson and come up with a new plan. It will take resilience to make your dreams come true.

Habits That Promote Personal Development

1. Work Smarter, Not Harder

There's just not enough time to accomplish everything that we ever wanted to. Thus, to achieve our important life goals, we've got to work smarter, not harder. Being productive is not about how long you sit at your desk, but it has everything to do with how effective your methods are. The following are some tips on working smarter:

2. Set Daily Goals

Most of us have big dreams. We want to live like royalties. Although, the problem is that we have no plan on how to achieve these dreams, which ultimately costs us the dream. One of the methods of ensuring that we achieve our goals is by setting daily goals. The following are some tips on setting daily goals:

- Make a list of all your goals: First off, write down all the things that you want to achieve. Ensure that you capture precisely what you want from life. For instance, instead of saying, "I want to be an artist," you should say, "I want to be a pop singer." Go through your list and ensure that you have written down every goal that you have ever had. This will help you get into the mindset of a winner.

- Break down your goals: For instance, if you have a goal of becoming a TV show host, you cannot get there overnight. You have to work at it day by day until you eventually get there. So, ensure that you break down your goals into daily activities. For instance, if you want to become a successful singer, you can start by ensuring that every day you record a new song. The more you practice your craft, the more skilled you become, and this opens you up to opportunities. But you have to be reasonable while breaking down your goals so that you can stay true to yourself.

- Set deadlines: You should put a deadline for your goals so that you can be motivated to act. Deadlines will help you track your progress. If you fail to reach a certain milestone within a certain period, it means that you are falling behind, and you have to push yourself harder to accomplish your goal within the set time frame.

- Ensure that you are realistic: One of the biggest limitations of goal setting is coming up with unreachable goals. To avoid this problem, ensure that you are setting goals at a time when you are emotionally calm and stable. This will allow you to be objective and come with goals that you can achieve if you commit. Setting unrealistic goals will only blow up your ego, but when reality dawns on you, it can be a bitter pill to swallow, making you incredibly upset.

- They must be measurable: Ensure that you can measure to what extent you want to achieve. Ensure that you put down the quantity or quality of your goal. For instance, if you want to transform your image, you may say something along the lines of "I want to lose 20 pounds."

- Come up with routines: Routines help us stick to our habits. For instance, if you have a short-term goal of losing 20 pounds, you may have to perform workouts every day. Take note of your preferred time and stick to working out. By creating a routine, you won't even seem as though you are trying too hard, and you will be able to achieve your desired results in no time.

- Track your goals: If you have a goal that you are running towards, ensure that you have an estimate of how near you are from that goal. This will help you understand whether you are making progress or coming up short. If you are not making any progress, you might want to change your routine and ensure that you are using the methods that work.

- Take it a step at a time: Don't rush into things. Take your time to think things through. Ensure you have sufficient insight into what you are about to start. The more mentally prepared you are, the better for you.

3. Fight Away Procrastination

Nothing kills dreams faster than procrastination. So many capable people end up wasting their potential thanks to procrastination. And this negative habit stems from a mix of fear and laziness. But to achieve your dreams, you have to confront procrastination head-on, and see to it that you are always productive. The following are some tips on avoiding procrastination.

- Do it as the first thing: If you find yourself procrastinating a lot, it might be due to exhaustion, and if that's the case, then the answer is to perform the activity when you are filled with energy. Studies show that we are most energetic when we awaken from sleep. This is because sleep has refreshed our minds, and we are in a relaxed state. So, if there's an activity that you always keep pushing off, start doing it in the morning after breakfast, i.e., when you are filled with energy. It will become a habit of yours, and eventually, you won't have trouble with procrastination.

- Get someone to hold you accountable: If you are always procrastinating important activities because you are too consumed with your private pursuits, you might want to get someone who will hold you accountable. This is an individual that you respect and who understands the value of your dreams. This person will be checking up on your progress and reminding you to do the necessary. Sometimes you are not aware that you are sinking by the day in retrogressive habits until there's someone to point it out.

- Show commitment: Without commitment, you can hardly get around to accomplishing your goals. The conditions will not always be right for you. But if you are committed, you will be willing to push yourself harder, and see to it that you have achieved your goals. Showing commitment helps you develop the right discipline to succeed in life.

- Visualize your success: Visualizing is the practice of seeing your success through your mind's eye. Through visualizing, you can see where you want to be, and it motivates you to take the necessary actions so that you succeed. So learn to use visualization to fight away procrastination.

Chapter 3

Positive Thinking: Big Scam, Miracle Solution or Real Tool?

Have you ever noticed how some things can divide the population, while others do not? I was still very young when I first observed this phenomenon. At the time, I was attending a wrestling show (I was a big fan at the time...) I don't know if you've ever watched a wrestling show, but before a fight, each participant makes his entrance: music, video on the big screen, the whole thing! I still remember the sound of the crowd cheering for its heroes! At least for a small part of them. Many of the wrestlers did not receive a standing ovation. Only the most loved or hated would trigger a reaction in the crowd. I had no idea that I had just witnessed one of the greatest marketing principles: Successful people trigger as much admiration as hatred, but in both cases, they trigger something. Whereas something average triggers nothing. Why would I tell you about this memory? Well, it's very simple: Just as successful wrestlers unleash the crowds, positive thinking leaves no one indifferent. Some people talk about it as a quick fix, others as a big scam. The truth probably lies somewhere in between. Indeed, being positive takes effort! And not everyone likes it. Some people want to change their lives with positive thinking, start a few exercises, and stop after a few days, simply because they didn't think they had to make an effort. So when they see testimonials on the Internet, instead of questioning themselves, they question the concept of positive thinking. But don't get me wrong. Positive thinking works and can change your life if you give it enough time and effort.

Thus, more than a simple tool or method, I see positive thinking as a state of mind. You will soon discover it in this: There is no half measure. Either you are positive, with the right state of mind, or you are not! So my question is, do you want to acquire the power of positive thinking? More importantly, why do you want to be positive? This question may seem stupid to you, who wouldn't want to be after all? Yet not everyone is. As I said before, being positive will take some effort on your part. If you're not ready for that, no one can help you. You might as well save yourself some time and stop reading that now. On the other hand, if deep down you want to make a real change and more color in your life, then this will be a great help.

Still here? Perfect! Let's attack the sinews of war: Negative thoughts.

Negative Thoughts: The Sinews of War

Why do we have negative thoughts?

When I talk about positive thinking, this question often comes up: But Arnaud, why do we have negative thoughts? If they are so harmful, why do they exist?

That's an interesting question. After all, it would be easier if we were all positive, wouldn't it?

I may shock you, but if we were all positive by nature, none of us would be here to talk about it anymore. Our species would have been extinct long ago!

Let me explain: Being happy is only a secondary goal for human beings. Indeed, the main objective of any species is to survive.

And do you think positive thinking would have allowed us to survive? Far from it!

Let's take an example: Imagine yourself in the time of prehistoric man. In those days, we didn't think about happiness.

The simple question we had was: Will I survive today or not?

Those who fared better were those who saw the future pessimistically. Those who envisioned that a bear might be behind the rock survived when it did.

Imagine if your classmate says, *"Maybe there's a bear, but maybe not. Don't make a negative plan! You're going to be sad. We'll just have to check for ourselves!"*

You might be sad, but your chances of staying alive would be much higher.

The sad truth is this: Negative thinking is the only way of thinking that is capable of ensuring our survival.

Another example: He who thinks that everyone is plotting behind his back will not make friends, but will be attentive to the slightest attempt at betrayal. There was a time when it was better to pay attention than to make friends.

But all that has changed, and now our survival is no longer threatened. The problem is that despite the millennia that have passed, our brains have changed very little.

He keeps himself unconscious of negative thinking to ensure his survival. He doesn't care if his survival is no longer threatened; he persists in this way "just in case."

That's why being happy is a choice and practicing positive thinking takes effort: It's just not in our nature! When do they arise?

At the time, the fear of death directed all our actions.

Problem: Although dying is no longer our daily fear, we still have fears.

It manifests itself in various and varied forms: the fear of failure, the fear of being rejected, the fear of not being enough...

The brain makes no difference between these different fears. When fear arises, it turns on the machine and goes into survival mode. This deprives you of your rational side and triggers a surge of negative emotions.

That's why before an important appointment, you get much stressed: Your brain thinks you're in danger and does everything it can to stop you from going.

Among the techniques of our brain to deter us, we find two main families:

1 - Calling on past failed experiments

You have a date, but a few minutes before you leave, you remember the last date: It went so badly!

2 - Projecting ourselves into several unfavorable scenarios

How do you know the next one will be as good? Maybe he or she won't find you pretty, imagine if he or she doesn't come! And if it doesn't go well, what are you going to tell your friends?

The machine is switched on. You start to project yourself into a future that hasn't even happened and may never happen. But at the moment, you can't take that step back. With fear in your stomach, you send a message that something is wrong with you.

If it's ever happened to you, do you remember the relief? Your brain thought at that moment that you were going to die, but now you're finally out of the woods! That's a relief!

Except that a few minutes or hours later, the truth catches up with you: You would have liked to go... At that moment, tons of "modern" negative thoughts reach you:

- I am weak.

- I'm not brave.

- Anyway, nobody likes me.

- What's the point of getting in my head, I'll end up alone...

If you recognize yourself in these few examples, understand that these reactions are NORMAL. This is our nature.

On the other hand, now that you are aware of some of the brain's mechanisms, you have a responsibility to act so that you are no longer subject to these automatic reactions. As of today, you know the great trickery of the brain.

The consequences of negative thoughts

As you can imagine, negative thoughts have important consequences in our lives.

If you think that the examples cited are isolated cases, you should know that your brain has more than 60,000 thoughts every day, 80% of which are negative!

So trust me, your brain takes no rest when it comes to keeping you alive... And unhappy.

All these negative thoughts lead to, among other things:

- A bad mood.
- Stress (a modern adult word for fear...)
- A loss of flavor, even in the joyful moments of your life.
- Loneliness, because you are gradually closing yourself off...
- The icing on the cake: A total loss of confidence!

You've understood it. It's urgent to act! I don't wish anyone to go through this.

Enough about negative thoughts! I suggest you focus on positive thinking from now on.

To begin, here is a heartbreaking story of a young girl saved by positive thinking.

The Heartbreaking Story of Winnie Harlow Saved by Positive Thinking

Winnie Harlow was a girl like any other until she was four years old. At the age of four, doctors diagnosed her with skin disease: Vitiligo.

Simply put, Winnie's immune system sees melanin as a disease to be eradicated. Melanin is a biological pigment that determines the color of skin, hair, and eyes in particular.

Gradually, some white spots appear on Winnie's body, which rubs off with the rest of the body.

Her whole childhood, she's been on the outside looking in. Sometimes because of the mockery of the children, sometimes because of the ignorance of the parents, thinking that the disease was contagious.

All this mockery is forcing Winnie to change schools. But the scenario repeats itself over and over again, no matter what school.

After college, and after so much mockery, Winnie decides to do something about it.

At first, Winnie succumbs to his negative thoughts. Instead of being a victim, she becomes the executioner.

She notices every weakness and uses it to belittle others. She tells herself that if she can't be good enough for others, then no one else will be.

As you can imagine, nothing good happens when you abandon yourself to negative thoughts. Seeing that she was scaring people her own age even more, because of her wickedness, she decided to stop everything, to make a new start.

From that moment on, Winnie accepts the idea that this disease will be part of her life forever.

Instead of spreading evil, she chooses to practice positive thinking. After a lot of work on herself, she finds herself beautiful and manages to love herself.

Do you think that's the end of the story? Well, it doesn't!

To encourage people to love and accept each other more, she decides to be a symbol.

She eventually achieved her goal by becoming the face of the Residual brand. Not only does she accept her looks, but she uses them to her advantage. Winnie has turned her uniqueness into strength.

To date, Winnie is followed by almost eight million people on social networks.

Incredible, isn't it?

I have a question for you:

How would you have lived such a childhood?

If this disease was yours, what would you do with it? Would you fall like Winnie into negative thinking for a while, or would you stay there for the rest of your life?

We can ALL practice positive thinking. We can all become a source of inspiration to those around us, regardless of our background and circumstances.

The sooner you realize this, the quicker the changes in your life will happen.

I can hear from my chair the question that burns your lips:

I understand, Arnaud, but HOW to do it? How can I practice positive thinking too?

I'll give you ten powerful tips. If you apply them, they will allow you to, among other things:

1. Being happier.

2. Becoming a better person.

3. Chase away negative thoughts when they arise.

Chapter 4
Enjoy Your Empathy

Regardless of our empathic abilities or lack thereof, we all aim to fill our lives with as much joy as possible. The empath should find that their overall level of happiness generally increases. As it becomes easier to recognize and manage the different types of energies that surround them, it will also become easier to be selective and make consistently positive choices.

Still, even for those who have mastered these skills and choose to focus all of their energy on positivity, constant and everlasting joy is an unrealistic goal to strive for. We all have our blind spots, vulnerabilities, and weaknesses. Sooner or later, the empowered empath will encounter a source of negativity that they cannot (or simply do not wish to) ignore, compartmentalize, or remedy.

It is in those moments, where joy is not accessible, that the empath must learn to find a way to inner peace instead. Imagine, for example, that someone you love and deeply respect has passed away. It would be ludicrous for anyone, even an empowered empath, to expect to find their way to true joy during the funerary services, or at any point within the mourning period. Whatever your views on death and the possibility of an afterlife may be, a loss of this magnitude is always painful. If the empath wishes to attend a wake or funeral, they'll certainly need to prepare themselves for the experience. They have to utilize whatever strategies they need to avoid taking on the pain of other mourners in the room. However, the empath who is focused exclusively on seeking joy may run the risk of ignoring their genuine feelings of pain, thereby distancing the self from emotions and feelings that belong to no one else. This is a dangerous practice for any empath to grow accustomed to, as it can be seductively pleasant at first. But much like the alcoholic who avoids the pain of a hangover by consistently consuming the hair of the dog that bit them, the empath will find that they can never outrun their own emotions. Even if they aim to shut them out the same way that they shut out the feelings of negative people, the emotions almost always find their way back to the empaths.

Balance ultimately, is a superior goal. An empath with a strong sense of inner balance can attend a funeral, commiserate with others, honor their sadness, and process feelings of grief without being consumed by them. Their balance allows them to recognize that sadness is not an opposing force to happiness, but rather that it is a functional part of joy; that without misery, we would never feel bliss or perhaps anything at all.

Over time, the empath will learn that this state of equilibrium is indeed their most heightened state of being and the place where they will find their truest self.

Learn how to deal with discomfort

Here's a revolutionary idea that can take your yoga, tai chi, or mindfulness practice to the next level: Discomfort is just an emotion. It isn't real. It isn't a threat, but it is a motivator.

Embracing discomfort isn't the same as numbing yourself to it. When you accept cognitive dissonance or moral injustices, you numb yourself to discomfort, embracing apathy, and encouraging the distortion of the truth. When you allow yourself to experience discomfort without immediately reacting, however, you can learn to make empowered choices, overcome fears and anxieties, and reach towards emotional growth. For empaths, discomfort is often a sensation of uncertainty or anticipation of conflict. If you can learn to recognize the feeling without letting it trigger your fight or flight response, you can instead focus on taking productive action, making yourself the true master of your universe.

This is an enlightened position that very few humans take. If you can start to use your discomfort as a tool, rather than avoiding it at all costs, you may find yourself able to overcome challenges that leave others destroyed. Once you've mastered this technique, do your best to pay it forward to another empath.

- **Live a comfortable life**

One thing that can throw any empath off balance and block the pathway to inner peace is a lack of authenticity in your lifestyle. Empaths often carry lies or dishonesty inside for long periods, haunted by them, even allowing the memory of them to block their throat, heart, and solar plexus chakras. This being the case, empaths should avoid lying whenever possible--even white lies can cause disruptions in your energy field.

You can work towards this goal through both addition and elimination. Also, make a point to invite positive energy flow into your life by aligning your career, personal relationships, eating habits, and hobbies with your value system. For example, if you have come to realize that environmentalism is deeply important to you, then pursuing work in green planning would be a fantastic first step. You could also reach out to foster new friendships with people who are passionate about the same causes. You might alter your diet to favor organic, locally sourced produce, and make a heightened effort to buy from environmentally conscious companies.

For elimination, you'll want to start purging anything from your life that put you in a position of moral conflict. If your job or social circle is not environmentally conscious, you'll be under constant pressure to swallow your truth and project dishonesty, which will ultimately leave you feeling dissatisfied and ungrounded. Any relationship wherein you feel the need to lie to keep everyone happy is a bad relationship for you, and you should feel free to let go of it.

You'll also want to stop using your money to support brands whose values contradict your own, and give up any habits that harm the things that matter most to you—for instance, if you love poetry, songs, and other forms of vocal expression, it's maybe time to quit smoking cigarettes once and for all. You might be pleasantly surprised to notice your physical body and metaphysical energy shift in a tangible way once you release the cognitive dissonance you once held inside yourself. You'll feel lighter, taller, more dynamic, and more capable.

I'll include another reminder here to be careful with social media use. Sometimes, these applications can do a lot of good to bring people together and inject dynamic momentum into progressive movements—but most often, they are cesspools of inauthentic energy. Aim to use these platforms sparingly, if at all, and to post honestly and responsibly.

- **Choosing Humility and Respecting the Unknown**

No matter how empowered one may become, and regardless of how well one has honed their empathic power, it is important to embrace humility and keep the mind open for unexpected possibilities. The self-righteous empath who develops a hermetic view of the world, unwilling to entertain ideas that do not strongly resonate with their interior knowledge, is likely to be deeply dissatisfied or anxious, and struggle with communication and loving relationships, as others will perceive them to be arrogant and standoffish.

This type of attitude is also likely to weaken your empathic powers. Truth is multifaceted and always changing. To grasp even a sliver of it, the empath must maintain a balanced connection between their interior and exterior worlds. Shutting either out, or favoring one over the other, will eventually lead the empath to receive misleading messages, or lead them to misinterpret messages that would otherwise be clear and easy to decipher. Empaths are privy to knowledge that often goes unseen, unheard, unacknowledged. Still, from time to time, they can be flat out wrong, especially if the information they're receiving from the exterior world is limited, it can be skewed to support an incomplete hypothesis.

There is an ancient Indian parable, of possible Buddhist origin, that has become popular in discussions of philosophy and religion, spreading to cultures throughout the world and retold in several different versions, about a group of blind men who encounter an elephant in the jungle. (Perhaps this parable is due for a modern update to include an equal number of blind women. Please bear in mind. Men are not the only gender susceptible to the pitfalls this proverb warns us against.) In this story, each of the blind men must use only their hands to try and comprehend the elephant's size, shape, and overall nature; however, one man's hands find only the elephant's tusks, while another finds only the rough skin of a hind leg, and another still can only feel the animal's wide, thin ears. When they compare their experiences, they are each convinced that the others are wrong or insane; in some versions of the story, this inability to agree on their sensory perceptions leads the men to resort to violence. Ultimately, the point of the story, which only the audience can see, is that each of the blind men is right, describing his experience accurately and honestly; the only problem is that they fail to acknowledge the perspectives of others as equally valid.

This is human nature, though the parable aims to inspire us to evolve past it. The truth can never be fully comprehended from one fixed vantage point. It is far too vast for any single person to hold alone. Still, the enlightened empath will be more successful than most at gathering contrasting perspectives and finding a way to incorporate them all into a single philosophy or belief, untangling knots of cognitive dissonance and drawing connections between seemingly disparate concepts. If, and only if, they are willing to stay humble and open to uncomfortable experiences that is. This pursuit should be handled with care—again, there is a difference between mild discomfort and decisively negative energy. And the empath needs to stay guarded against the latter. Don't force yourself to endure an experience that is depleting rather than charging you, but don't let yourself fall into the habit of avoiding the challenging and unpredictable opportunities life offers you, either. As an example, many empaths learn early in their journey to self-empowerment that large crowds can quickly cloud or drain their energy fields. They may have had one particularly difficult or painful experience at a party, concert, funeral, wedding, or rally, and quickly decide that it would be best to avoid large gatherings from that point on. This might be a mistake, though, as joining large groups that are unified in honest intention (a faith-based service, or performance that is effective at steering the emotional path of every audience member, for example) can be one of the most positive and energizing experiences available to the empath.

Though it may be tempting to stay cocooned in whatever emotional spaces feel safer, the empath must make a point of continuously expanding their perspective by trying new things, meeting new people, and seeking out challenges for the sake of growth. The most important thing for any empath to know is just how much the universe has yet to teach them.

Chapter 5

Mental Toughness - High Frustration Tolerance

Would we change who we are, what we feel, and also how we behave? Can a leopard change its spots? I recently talked to somebody who asked if a psychologist is just painting over the spots of the "leopard," and underneath, we all stay the same. Okay, I don't see many leopards in my consulting room, but I see people still shifting. A positively changed mindset is important for cognitive strength and resilience.

The fundamental difference between a leopard, a dog, a tree, and a human being is that other living things have already figured out their course and purpose. A leopard will become a leopard; a tree will do what a tree does. The manual for directions is included.

It is our duty to us human beings, who and what we are in every moment. We are self-conscious and self-determined. We are dropped into the world with no script or stage directions as actors on a stage. We don't have a manual of instructions. That is why our responsibility is who we are and what we become. Of course, some factors affect who we are today, how I have mentioned above, but the important point I am trying to make in this regard is that these factors cannot be overused as excuses for our future.

Family and culture: What we are could be said to be the product of our education and community. We may have accepted messages and information from other people and the world about ourselves. For example, because we are "lazy," "no good," "good for nothing," or "not expected to succeed," we may have accepted ideas about others that are unintelligent or barbarous, mean, and controlled. We may think that the world is typically dangerous, carefree, or unfriendly. The fact is these ideas could have been kept alive and continued to be accepted uncritically and not reassessed. If we did, then this is our decision, and we must continue to believe it.

DNA and genetics: In terms of our DNA and genetics, we have a little selection. 50% of our parents and 25% of each grandparent are the heritage. We may be more open to some sports and activities, although we will only do that if we have the right tuition and mentoring. We can also inherit physical and mental illness predispositions. Our genes may have an impact, but we are not dogs and racehorses in pedigree shows, we are self-aware freethinking people, and still, determine what our future is at every time.

You are pushed through the atmosphere. Sometimes, it is implied that we are already a reflection of our society and that you will improve the individual when you change the environment. Consider these examples: When you stop homelessness, you can stop crime because when people are poor, they commit crimes. It will be rehabilitated when you punish a thief and praise him for positive actions. The oppressed are "no choice," but terrorists. Teach a young man to play table tennis, and he will give up the sale of drugs and knife his opponents. I think you will agree that life is not that easy, and in their world, people still have choices.

We are driven by inner drives. Are we only at the mercy of our internal drives like drives for fun, energy, and meaning? We are not always rational, conscious people. In our thoughts and actions, our subconscious drives and desires for enjoyment, heat, comfort, physical contact, and gender control. The new field of evolutionary psychology, which explores our actions from the advantages of our ancestors, argues that many of our unconsciousness drives aim at gaining an evolutionary benefit and transmitting our genes. So, we are driven by evolution as well. We are also motivated by our need to influence and our attempts to be superior. For one field, we can compensate for our shortcomings by mastering another and being guided by subconscious objectives. For example, if we are unsuited to sports, we can excel in music. We can also strive to find meaning in conscious life goals and things like work and family. We still have control and responsibility for our lives by understanding these drives and instincts.

And after all of the above, should we change our free will?

I believe you know my answer. When we accept that we are the result of our creation, culture, genetics, the environment, psychology, and evolution, we are only the victims of external influences and internal conditions. As people, we have the right to stand and change beyond our climate and circumstances at all times.

A leopard can't change his spots because he's a leopard, but you can pinch your issues and turn them into goals. Take the idea that the past is all-important; we all have a history, but we must not be the past.

Living a Healthy Life

LONGEVITY: Long-life and great health can be significantly promoted by our nutritional (most important) and physical activities, such as regular exercise.

Regulations and health habits: 1st rule: eat less, and live longer?

Calorie restriction has been one of the strongest measures to control aging, but it is a significant controversy.

Experiments have shown that underfed rodents live 40% longer than their healthy counterparts. The same findings for fruit flies, worms, apes, and other experimental laboratories have been published.

One obvious fact about this is that it's quite a hard task to deal with calories because people who have experienced it will quickly expose themselves to you.

Studies on people who use calorie intake limits found that some aging predictor, e.g., blood glucose rates, blood pressure, cholesterol, etc., all improved on CR diets.

Because of the challenges facing people trying to limit their calorie intake, the goal is now to find drugs that can give people all the advantages of calorie restriction without diets.

The resveratrol exists in many forms of life and is released from the body system by pressure. This slows down age when the activity of a molecule called SRT1 is intensified. It explains how the calorie restrictions work, and the body feels a persistent, mild pressure when starving so that it can defend against any more extreme stresses that may cause the cells to get older, i.e., the body cells, to protect themselves from further decay.

If resveratrol could be supplied in the form of tablets, then the body could have succeeded in manipulating itself, believing that it receives not enough calories and then the body's reactions are aimed at defending itself against further deterioration and thus slowing down aging, but this is still an idea that researchers are exclusively interested in now.

Eat Right when you look.

People prefer to eat junk food than to eat the right kind of food and thus dig their early tombs in ignorance.

An average individual presently would have adjusted to the life of fast food joints in the morning, afternoon, and night. Others feel that more expensive cousins add more value to their meat. We do not know that there are many drawbacks to a big rice bowl with a salad dressing plus a big turkey lap, etc., that make up a meal for a person when retailed in fast-food joints that could predispose one to illnesses such as diabetes, cancer and many types of heart diseases. Remember some of the issues you might experience.

The intake of a lot of highly processed foods wouldn't satisfy you for a long time and would make you quickly return to more food so that you eat even more than you would need for a day.

The highly prepared food lacks the necessary vitamins to nourish life because many vitamins are water-soluble. In contrast, others are heat-labile, and so about 80% of the total vitamin contents of the food must have been depleted at a later stage of the processing. Always note that some of these vitamins are called vitamins of fundamental importance because our bodies cannot synthesize them.

Turkey's laps are full of cholesterol, the main cause of atherosclerosis, heart attack, and stroke is high in saturated fat.

The majority of preservatives used in highly processed foods are harmful to the human system (alien). Some are medications that can be converted into harmful metabolites after entering the body, while others have toxic effects when they enter the body.

Most processed foods are colored to make them more attractive to the eyes by adding chemicals. Such additives are typically not licensed by most of the food authorities and should not be used in food preparations.

To avoid these problems mentioned and to achieve a healthy age and longevity, you are advised to always feast on fruit and vegetables.

Which fruit and vegetable products?

Not only are fruits and vegetables good for you, but also they are far too good because they contain several phytochemicals that induce longevity.

What are phytochemicals?

Some are also referred to as supplements. Evidence combined with life evidence indicates that these chemicals help restore good health and quality of life and sustain a long life. We function by removing free radicals that are highly reactive species that are produced by living processes and that cause constant damage to cells and tissues of the body. Sources and their roles of phytochemicals are:

a) Flavonoids; they are naturally grown from citrus fruits, onions, apples, and grapes. A class of phytochemicals is supposed to protect against cancer and other diseases of degeneration. An apple a day for flavonoids helps to prevent cancer. Attach citrus fruit, for example. The oranges and grapes are used to generate variegations and to establish variegations so that you have an interest in your fruit and vegetables and not a monotone apple a day that soon can be of value.

b) Carotenoids make your oranges look orange, give your banana a yellow look, and give your carrots color. They also become vitamin A in your skin. Lutein, zeaxanthin, and Lycopene protect against cataracts, against coronary artery diseases, cancer, and against muscle degeneration – all further justification for eating carotenoids.

c) Apples, fiber, grapes, carrots, and bananas are considered to be very high in soluble and water -dissolving fiber. This pushes appetite back by limiting digestion and thus helps to reduce calories and ultimately to age. Rich diets with fiber are advised to combat heart disease, diabetes, obesity, cancer, and high blood pressure, all of which contribute to life elongation.

d) Are flavones, it is understood that certain plant chemicals replicate female natural hormones known to decrease, such as estrogen, in menopausal women. The crop estrogen is a rich source of flavones phytochemical. The use of is flavones can provide many benefits, such as lower levels of blood lipid, relief from menopausal symptoms and reduced breast cancer predisposition, ovarian cancer, endometrial cancer, and prostate cancer.

e) Switch: Switch your concentration with something as simple as fluffing pillows on the sofa, open blinds all over the house, plug in a laundry wash or check your email or text messages... Get out of the kitchen! Get out of the kitchen!

Avoidable trigger: If you are used to snacking every day at a certain time, adjust your routine, so you do an activity.

Chapter 6
Habits, Rituals & Daily Practices

The Power of Self-Love

Self-love is extremely important when developing positive self-talk and integrating it into daily life. This is because self-talk, as you are aware, is about the conversations you have with yourself and the stories you tell yourself are true. Self-love, therefore, is essential.

Self-love and self-talk can almost be seen to be synergistic. Without self-love, the conversations we have with ourselves would lack the love, compassion, and kindness we deserve. If we do not love ourselves, how can we possibly expect to love others or engage in positive thinking? Love can be seen as the essence of life itself.

Also, to kindness and compassion, having a love for you enhances respect. Without self-respect, we tend to attract negative, detrimental, and harmful situations and interactions in our lives. Our energy fields become polluted with other people's stories, illusions, harms, and intents, which can be very destructive if we have not set the necessary barriers and boundaries to protect ourselves from them. Self-love can help us do this.

As the power of gratitude, self-love also acts as a force. Al the feelings, thoughts, and associations are amplified when we engage in and connect to self-love and project it both internally and externally. *Love is a powerful vibration*, and some of the most awe-inspiring, extraordinary, and unbelievable miracles have occurred through love.

So, how do we practice self-love and integrate it daily? Fortunately, the ways are many! Let's explore a few essentials for now.

1. ***Follow your passions!*** Staying committed to your goals and dreams is an integral self-love practice. Often we can appease others and adopt a "people-pleasing" attitude. This is especially true if you are highly empathic, sensitive, or suffer from feelings of depression and lack of self-worth and confidence. Remaining focused and aligned to your own goals and dreams, therefore, naturally provides you with the self-love necessary for a healthy and positive mindset. What good are we to the world at large if we allow others to bring us down with their negativity, cynicism, or judgment? Staying true to your passions will help greatly.

2. ***Spend time in nature.*** Spending time in nature could be one of the most powerful things you do for yourself. In nature, we are refreshed, re-energized, and rejuvenated. Our emotions are restored, and our mental frame of mind is cleared. Nature is deeply healing and connecting with the natural world, and all its elements will have incredible results for both your self-love and positive self-talk.

3. ***Look after your health.*** Looking after your health is self-love, in essence. Health is not just physical but also mental, emotional, and spiritual. We are holistic beings, and all of

our bodies interact with each other. We are designed to maintain homeostasis just as the earth is designed to achieve balance, equilibrium, and wholeness. Practicing self-love by taking care of your health can have a profound effect on all aspects of life and thinking.

4. ***Strengthen your boundaries!*** Make a conscious effort to engage in daily exercises and techniques that will increase your boundaries and, therefore, your love for yourself. Having healthy boundaries can act as a shield against your negative thinking and the harmful thoughts and projections of others.

5. ***Practice forgiveness.*** There is nothing more self-loving than practicing forgiveness. Whether it is for self or others, forgiveness keeps you in a state of love and compassion as you are releasing all that no longer serves. Like journaling, you are allowing yourself to let go, heal, and release, therefore, cleansing your energy field and energetic space for the attraction of new opportunities, moments, and connections. Holding on to things that cause you pain and suffering is not self-loving and is, therefore, not healthy for positive self-talk. Be kinder to yourself through forgiveness.

The Power of Self-Care

Like self-love, self-care is intrinsically tied to self-talk and positive thinking. How can we possibly be centered and aligned to a path of clear and healthy thinking if we are not looking after ourselves? Self-care can take many forms as the self is such a complex and holistic entity.

Let's take a deeper look at how self-care can be applied in everyday reality.

Self-healing, healing massage, and other self-loving rituals. Self-healing, healing massage and other self-loving rituals are prime examples of self-care. These are your traditional pampering sessions, which you know make you feel good. Expanding slightly, however, and subsequently having a profound effect on thinking positively, is the intention of remembering and being aware of the holistic nature of these self-pampering activities. Massage and other forms of pampering aren't purely physical; they also affect the mind, emotions, and spiritual well-being. Engaging in activities daily, therefore, can lead to greater care, improved happiness and energy levels, and an advanced sense of confidence. This is because, when we are loving and caring ourselves, we are *feeling good*. Feeling good is the basis of positive thinking! (Although it is important to note the distinction between feeling good genuinely, sincerely, and purely as opposed to narcissistic, manipulative, or inauthentic forms of happiness.)

Develop your intuition. When we develop our intuition, our inner knowing, we can better take care of ourselves. Our whole self is designed to work in harmony and achieve a state of balance and wholeness. As our intuition is our ability to know things, connected to our gut and instincts, this ties in strongly. Engaging in activities and practices that strengthen intuition can lead to many positive results. These include making choices in alignment with the heart, higher self (the higher mind), and unified, conscious, and connected living and knowing when it is necessary to protect yourself from certain people, energies, and situations. Your intuition is essentially your guide to love, connection, protection, and bliss. Without self-care, intuition can become sacrificed, which harms the ability to think positively and keep thoughts and awareness aligned to higher values and intents.

Take time for meditation, reflection, introspection, and journaling. Taking time for these activities, also to exploring yourself and psyche, shadow and light, can help you develop a sense of care and aid in positive self-talk. Once again, the shadow is an integral part of the self, and we often have unconscious triggers, traumas, and wounds that influence us but that we are unaware of. Journaling, reflecting, and contemplating life can be very nourishing for the soul and healing for the mind. Look to your psyche, explore the world of dreams, and introspect on various aspects and memories that have shaped your life.

Create a sacred space. Creating a sacred space is a powerful self-care ritual, and it can easily be integrated into daily life. Create a shrine or altar and make sure it has a connection to all the elements, for example, a feather (air), a crystal or gemstone (earth), a candle (fire), and a shell or symbolic bowl of water (water). It also includes a sentimental or meaningful picture and some flowers or petals to enhance the effects.

This is because each of the objects described carries a unique vibration and specific frequency, and it is necessary to include them to receive their benefits and amplify the effects of our meditation, mantra, or daily ritual practice. These practices can include gratitude mantras affirmations, intention setting, meditating, and exercises to cultivate inner peace, compassion, and a positive daily mindset. Create a sacred space and see how your energy shifts throughout your day.

Eat healthily! Diet is very important for self-care and developing and maintaining a positive, healthy mindset. Food has an intrinsic effect on our well-being, our physical bodies, and our emotions. The foods we eat influence how we feel, think, and respond to certain situations. Food affects our psychological, physiological, mental, emotional, spiritual, and physical well-being, and eating foods with no nutrition, foods that are heavy and make us feel sluggish, or foods that contain toxins, chemicals, and harmful substances can drastically reduce our vibration. When we refer to vibration, we mean: all food types contain a life force, energy, and specific vibrational frequency. Foods high in life force, for example, include fruits, vegetables, whole grains, beans, lentils and pulses, herbs, nuts, and seeds. They receive their energy solely from the sun, air, earth, and water and, therefore, are created directly from a primary life force. They are also high in nutrients (as opposed to other primary cycle food types like pasta). Choosing to nurture and sustain ourselves, therefore, with the right foods can enhance positive thinking greatly and all the other forms of self-talk practices.

The Importance of Health on Mood

As explored already, health is extremely powerful in shaping, creating, and affecting mood, also to emotions and thought processes. Health, however, encompasses the following: diet, nutrition, exercise, movement, and mental, physical, and spiritual health. Each state of health affects the other – the entire self is interconnected. Enhancing any one of these areas, therefore, profoundly affects the others.

We will explore the power of exercise. Let's have a look at health from a holistic angle and delve slightly deeper into the significance of diet and nutrition.

Primary cycle foods vs. secondary cycle foods

Food is essentially energy with its own life force. A vegetable grows and is nurtured directly from the sun, air, rain, and the earth. It, therefore, absorbs all its energy and nutrients directly from the elements, directly from the source. In this sense, foods like vegetables can be seen to be in their *primary cycle*. They essentially hold a higher vibration due to their life force. Animals, on the other hand, are in their *second cycle* (or even third). When we eat animals, we are receiving our nutrients from a "third party." Animals are sustained through either plants and vegetation or other animals. This means that the life force energy of the crops has been diminished by the time we eat the animal. Instead of getting our energy, vitality, nutrition, and life force directly from primary-source food, we miss out on one or two important cycles. Every living thing has a life force, as everything is energy. Also, when we consume animals, we are consuming the pain and suffering stored in their cells. Let's take a moment to let that sink in. *We are consuming the pain and suffering stored in their cells!*

All cells hold memory, and we are fully aware that our thoughts, emotions, and feelings affect us on an intrinsic level. So, when we eat animals, we are also absorbing the energy of their trauma and suffering. Please note this information is not intended to offense (just like the myth that we are responsible for our own health!). However, the majority of animals that are killed nowadays are indeed killed in excess and suffer terribly. Consumerism is, unfortunately, for mass-scale meat production, and we do not live in communities where we raise an animal with love, and then end their life purely to get the sustenance we need. Animals have become a market. Associated with this are the pain and suffering we humans cause them. Referring back to diet and nutrition, we are sentient, empathic, and intuitive beings. We *feel* things and are supposed to live life with compassion and a sense of love and respect for others and all life on earth.

Chapter 7
Feeling Your Feelings

Many couples with good communication skills struggle with some form of a "feeling problem" that short-circuits their closeness. This was the case with Lloyd and Janice.

When I asked them why they were seeking therapy, Lloyd responded, "Our communication is ninety-five percent on target. But that last five percent is affecting everything else."

As a diplomat, Janice was especially good at being aware of the nuances of people's spoken and unspoken needs and agendas. She exuded authority and self-confidence, though she had an abrupt way of changing the subject in a conversation that could be off-putting and intimidating. Lloyd ran his own life insurance company. His employees liked and respected him. He had a quirky sense of humor and a humble, soulful presence.

Lloyd described one of his major communication frustrations with Janice as the way she spoke to him when she wanted a task completed.

"Can you give an example?" I asked.

"Like when she tells me to put my shoes in the closet instead of in the foyer."

"How else should I say it?" Janice wondered aloud. "That's where shoes go."

"Do you ever tell Lloyd how seeing the shoes in the foyer make you feel?" I asked.

Janice looked at me askance—as though deciding whether or not to take me seriously.

"How it makes me feel?" she said. "To see his shoes?"

"Are you angry when you see them? Anxious?" I persisted.

Janice chuckled, still on the fence about taking me seriously. "I'm not sure I'm anything," she said. "We're talking about shoes here. But you know, maybe I do feel a bit anxious if stuff like that is out of place."

When we followed this thread—Janice's anxiety about household items or shoes being out of place—back through her history, we learned more about her problem with feelings.

Janice believed the best communication happened when feelings weren't involved. As the only child of two older and highly protective Dutch parents, she'd grown up in the center of their world. They'd tried to safeguard her from the pain of all kinds, including painful emotions like sadness, inadequacy, and embarrassment. Her parents' overprotectiveness hadn't saved her from these emotional experiences, though it *had* fostered shame about her feelings and led her to believe she had to cope with them on her own.

As she got older, Janice developed mechanisms for avoiding her feelings, called defenses. Psychologically speaking, defenses are strategies we practice, most often unconsciously, to protect ourselves from fear emotional experiences. In accelerated experiential dynamic psychotherapy (AEDP), a feeling and relationship-based therapy model developed by psychologist and author Diana Fosha, clients are encouraged to access the widest array of emotional and relational options available to them that have gone untapped or underutilized. Janice minimized the importance of her emotions. She also kept herself busy with a fierce, tunnel-vision focus on goals and tasks, neutralizing her emotions before they emerged.

"I need to know you're vulnerable," Lloyd said. It had touched him when Janice admitted to her problems with feelings. "It's good when you're not so put together."

"Do you like me better when I'm a hot mess," Janice joked.

"Much better," Lloyd said, smiling. "I like you when you're human."

How we deal with our feelings influences how much of our emotional reality we allow ourselves to inhabit. It shapes how comfortable we can get with all of our emotions, from ecstasy to grief, shame to pride, fear to love.

Regena Thomashauer, the founder of The School of Womanly Arts and a leading expert in modern feminism, writes in her blog "The 4 Keys to an Extraordinary Life" that life is better when we "play all 88 keys on our piano, not just Middle C, over and over again." For Janice, being an orderly perfectionist in control of every detail in her life was a defense against her own messy vulnerability. She'd been playing Middle C over and over again, limiting the full range of her emotional aliveness.

Exercise

The Speaker names each of the following feelings slowly and consciously, taking a moment to pause and notice how they feel after each word:

🗨 Happy.

🗨 Powerful.

🗨 Peaceful.

🗨 Sad.

🗨 Angry.

🗨 Scared.

What associations arise when you say, "happy," versus when you say, "Angry"? Look at the following Feeling Wheel. Are there offshoots of these feelings you hardly ever feel? If so, name them. Are there feelings you feel all the time, but keep to yourself? If so, name them.

Feeling Wheel

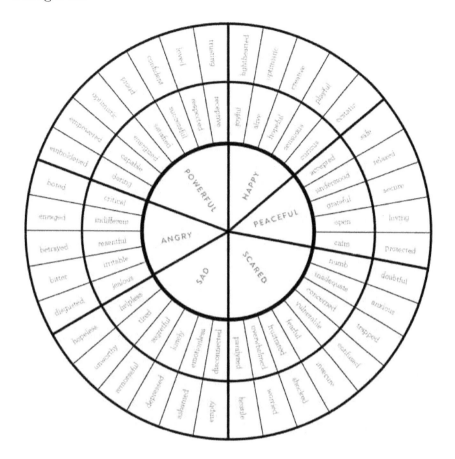

Sample Exchange:

SPEAKER: When I say the word "happy," I feel sad. There's a sense of loss and exhaustion. I'm always pursuing happiness rather than just feeling whatever I'm feeling, being wherever I am, and being okay with that. I have no problem feeling joy, pride, and sadness. I have a hard time feeling anger and helplessness. I'm aware that I cry a lot, so I guess crying is easy for me. My mom always cried, no matter what she felt. I think there's frustration under my tears.

LISTENER: Thank you for giving me this window into your inner world. It's helpful to know more about the different ways you experience your feelings.

To rewrite a story, you first need to know it's a story.

The Stories We Tell Ourselves

Gabriella and Jack were in their late thirties. They were both the eldest in their big immigrant families, Italian for Gabriella, and Irish for Jack. Each of them was also the first for whom the luxury of a college education had been possible. Gabriella was a tax attorney, and Jack was a New York City detective. They'd been living together for a decade, but they both agreed they'd been growing apart for a long time.

"It started a year and a half ago," Jack said. "After your hysterectomy."

When Gabriella first sat down, she had looked as though she was on the verge of tears, but when Jack spoke, she sat bolt upright in her chair. Her eyes narrowed with hostility.

"Because we stopped having sex," she said. "That's why you think it started a year and a half ago. Jesus, I swear, sex is all you care about, isn't it?"

Jack's face took on a shell-shocked expression.

"Let's back up," I said, sensing we'd just taken the first step into a well-trodden and unhelpful rabbit hole. "Gabriella, I'm going to coach you to say that again, only this time, see if you can take full responsibility for your assumptions."

"It's not an assumption," Gabriella insisted. "I know he watches porn. We don't have sex, so it's like I don't exist for him. He just goes into the basement when he comes home."

"The story I make up is that all you care about is sex," I coached.

"Are you kidding? You want me to repeat that?" Gabriella asked her face incredulous.

Stories are one of the biggest love-drains in relationships. Prefacing our assumptions with a simple phrase like *the story I make up* can release the death grip of a powerful story. For Gabriella, introducing her judgments of Jack as a *story* about him rather than an objective truth was a way of acknowledging that he was his own person with his own reality.

Gabriella sighed and turned to Jack.

"The story I make up is that all you care about is sex," she said reluctantly.

"And the way that story makes me feel is . . ." I coached, indicating that this was her next line in the script to try out and complete in whatever way felt more authentic to her.

"And the way that story makes me feel is . . . disgusted and angry."

"And when I feel disgusted and angry, I come by . . ."

A look of comprehension shifted the muscles around the Gabriella's mouth and eyes. "If I'm completely honest, I cope by making up *more* stories about how little you care about me, how men can't be trusted.

Then I bite your head off when you walk in the door."

Gabriella looked genuinely pleased with herself. It can be a relief when a person sees that they are the birthplace of their relationship horror stories, not their partner. If a potential intruder in a dark room turns into a coat rack when you switch on the light, your sense of safety and ease can be quickly and automatically restored.

Now Jack's eyes were moist.

"Okay, I guess I see why that would not be fun to come home to, and why you might avoid me when you walk in the door," Gabriella said.

Jack shrugged, looking sheepish.

Human beings are storytellers. It's how we make sense of the world. We tell ourselves stories because we're trying to make sense of situations that confuse us, and that's nothing to be ashamed of. Still, it helps to acknowledge that we do this and recognize when our stories become distortions of reality. Figuring out why our partners react the way they do take patience and humility. We may assume they think or feel like us, or that they act for similar reasons. Making assumptions is often easier than asking our partners what they are feeling or thinking. Asking instead of assuming allows us to learn about our partners from the only person who *knows* them: them!

Seeing, challenging, and interrupting your own horror stories about your mate, as Gabriella did with Jack, can turn intruders into coat racks and reconnect you with what's truly there.

Exercise

The Speaker identifies two of their most familiar stories (see the following "Common Horror Stories" list), then shares situations where these stories frequently pop up in their relationship. What do you feel about yourself, your partner, and your relationship when you believe these stories? How do you cope or react?

COMMON HORROR STORIES

- I'm not good enough.
- I can't get it right.
- I'm broken.
- I'm not lovable.
- I can't trust anyone.
- I'll always be alone.
- I don't fit in.
- I'm too old for love.
- I'm not important to you.
- I'm doomed to failure.
- Everyone abandons me.

- My needs don't matter.

- I'm too much.

- I'll never be fulfilled.

- I'm worthless.

- People always take advantage of me.

Sample Exchange:

SPEAKER: One of my relationship horror stories is that I can't get anything right. I tell myself this story whenever you ask where I put the car keys in a frustrated voice. It makes me feel hopeless and inadequate. I cope by withdrawing and withholding affection and telling myself other horror stories, such as that we'll never make it as a couple. When I choose to believe these stories, I feel angry and sad. I cope by pouring myself a glass of wine or spending hours shopping on the Internet.

LISTENER: Thank you for recognizing your relationship, horror stories, and owning up to them. It frees both of us up to know that they're just stories, and they don't have to define us as a couple.

Chapter 8
How to Stop Absorbing negative energies.

Empathy is a person's ability to recognize and understand the emotions of the people around him. But often being empathic means also absorbing a significant amount of suffering and pain in your environment, which at some point becomes a problem - both for the emotional state of the person and for his or her functioning as a whole. Do you think about Stephen King's novel "The Green Road" or the movie starring Michael Clark Duncan? His character, John Coffey, who has the extraordinary ability to "take away" the pain of the sufferer and heal him with the power of his own faith, says: "I'm tired of people acting so ugly with each other. I'm tired of the pain that I hear and feel the world every day. It's too much. I feel it as a piece of glass in my head..."

We all sometimes feel that way... Of course, there is no higher form of humanity than compassion and empathy. Still, it is imperative to learn how not to "absorb" the toxic energy that is often abundant around us.

Here are five ways to help keep bad energy away:

Remember: It is impossible to please everyone

When someone dislikes us and constantly complains about us, it is often our reaction to try to change our attitude and opinion. But this is a mistake. Don't make it the Mission of your life - it will only complicate things. The effort to please and prove yourself will only increase your dependence on that person's opinion of you. Accept the fact that we cannot be liked and appreciated by everyone, and remind yourself often that self-esteem and belief in our capabilities is our primary protection against the negative energy of others.

On the other hand, put up that you can't change them all, you can't "make them out" to your liking, nor is it possible to make them better or solve their problems. Put a barrier, and don't make it your mission.

Choose carefully the people you accept in your life

The body, our mind and the environment that surrounds us is our temple. Do you carefully select the people you allow into it, or are your doors always wide open?

In Brazil, there is a special word for such people - "Delgado," which means "lazy" in direct translation, but is used to mean "food that hangs on your neck." The point is this: If we give someone a piece of bread today, tomorrow he will ask us whole, if we invite someone to stay for the weekends, he will want to stay a whole week, even two. Of course, this is not about how good we are and how strong we desire to help; it is about having to be extra careful when someone overdoes our kindness. If you do not put the "thin red line," these types of people will continue to abuse your generosity and kindness, setting you up with a trap that would prevent you from helping someone who needs you. Just learn to say "NO" without worrying about it.

Make sure you don't pay attention

There are people who, because of their effect on us, can logically be described as "energy vampires." According to psychologist Sergei Klyuchnikov, in the modern world, they are four basic psychological types, the common thing between them being that they are just like parasites - to survive, they need a host. When we pay too much attention to someone, we are giving it our energy. What we focus on becomes greater, which is normal if a person tries to engage us in intrigue and constantly "nurture" our conviction for such, at one point, we seem to be living in reality created by him. Have you ever been tormented for days by the gossip or intrigue that is not worth your attention, but you feel like it makes you sick? This is exactly the impact of energy vampires. Of course, some are just passing by - pouring out their bad guys and moving on to their next stop.

Put in your "thin red line" in your relationships with friends who seem to want to "infect" you with negativity and bad experiences. A simple example: "I'm in love!" - "Oh, forget it (you), you will suffer, there is no love…"

Again, to be able to "exclude" others requires self-esteem and self-belief. To repel toxic energy, you have every right to tell someone to stop as rude as it sounds.

Turn nature into your friend

Walk more often, relax, breathe - breathing is one of the best ways to purify your body and mind from toxic energy.

Take 100 percent responsibility for your emotions and feelings

How we feel is our sole responsibility. Always remember that the perception we have of ourselves is far more powerful and valuable than what others have for us. We are not victims, and no one has authority over us. Think about how your own thoughts and emotions affect the situation that bothers you so much. The answer may lie in your level of tolerance, irritability, or compassion. If we are not vigilant, in practice, it will turn out as if we affirm that we are victims of the world around us. But when we begin to hold ourselves accountable for how we react to something, we connect with ourselves on a deeper level. Put yourself in situations that increase your energy - does it make you feel good, but how do you influence yourself? We all can recognize emotions, both our own and those we provoke in others. Learning to protect ourselves from the toxic energy of others is a long process that begins with self-love.

Stop trying always to please others

When someone complains about you or tries to ruin your mood, do not take it personal. Rather, this type of behavior is a reflection of what other people are and does not benefit you in any way. The more you respond to gossip and other people's opinions, the more dependent you become on the praise of others. It is essential to realize that you cannot make everyone like you, and those things that are valuable to you are not related to the opinions of others. Love yourself first, and don't let people who are trying to influence you get too close.

Beware of energy vampires

Have you had any friends who suck your life force? Friends that make you feel emotionally and physically drained? Precisely this type of person is an energy vampire. Such people always find a way to reach you when they need help, but you can never rely on them when you need them. And the more they complain, the more new things they come up with to complain about. In these situations, you need to remind yourself that it is not your responsibility to deal with another person's problems, even when it comes to a family member. If they cannot help themselves, it makes no sense for you to bear their burden. This will in no way help them and positively will not affect you good.

Learn to say NO

It is important to set certain limits and maintain them when they are violated. Learn to say NO when needed. Don't let anyone walk around with "dirty feet" in your mind. Do not let your self-esteem be harmed. Contrary to popular belief, it is not rude to say NO to anyone, and you do not need to seek an excuse for using that word. If you feel that the other side is not respecting you enough, stand up for yourself so that they hear and understand you. Your time and feelings are invaluable, so keep positive people around you and avoid the negative ones. If you find that you are saying NO to a "friend" more often than YES, then you should seriously consider whether you should continue to contact that person.

Take the time you need for yourself

Whether it's taking a bath or lazy bedtime in the morning, take the time to listen to your own inner voice. If you are in a noisy place and you cannot concentrate, take a walk outside in nature. Fresh air and plants will help you calm down. Whatever personal problem you may have, it is too small for the scale of the universe, and life always goes on. Enjoy the pure energy of the world around you and reconnect with your true self.

Learn to take responsibility

After all, you are the only person who determines how you feel. No matter what environment you are in, you always have the choice of staying strong or letting others exercise their authority over you. Remember to always be positive in your daily routine. Of course, sometimes negative thoughts will pop into your mind. You need to survive them and continue to live without them. When you have negative thoughts, do not be shy about crying as well, because this is the best medicine.

Chapter 9
How to Make Good Achievement Driven Habits

A long time ago, when Jerry Seinfeld was still on the comedy circuit, a younger comedian approached him for counsel on the best way to improve. Seinfeld answered that the way to being a better entertainer was composing better jokes, and the best approach to compose better jokes was to rehearse. In any case, it wasn't just about rehearsing, Seinfeld clarified; it was tied in with working up a habit: the composting habit.

Seinfeld proposed using a simple stunt to get the habit of moving. You purchase a large calendar with a crate for each day of the year. At that point, every day that you complete your composing task, you put a significant cross on the schedule. As the weeks pass, the chain of crosses on the schedule gets longer and longer. Your central goal, asked Seinfeld, was not to break the chain.

These sorts of stories contain a seed of truth about creating another habit, as do numerous bits of the lives of highly successful people. It's the reason they're so exciting: we sense that this day by day schedules conceal some significant mystery about how to accomplish the enormity of the success they had achieved. After looking into it further, we find that their everyday schedules are frequently and significantly simple; in some exceptional cases, individuals accomplish extraordinary things by working consistently towards their objectives.

Take one of the most persuasive scientific personalities ever, Charles Darwin. As per his son's testimony, Darwin's regular daily routine was metronomic in his early and later years. He rose at 7 am, ate breakfast alone, and then worked on his investigation from 8 am until 9:30 am, during which time he completed his best work. At that point, he broke for an hour's letter reading before coming back to his examination for a further 90 minutes work. The remainder of his day was taken up with strolling, eating, reading, letter composition, and family matters.

On the other hand, take the incredible comic author P. G. Wodehouse, maker of Jeeves and Wooster and the Blanding's Castle s. Wodehouse rose at 7:30 am, did his "every day dozen" calisthenics, ate (tea, toast, and espresso cake), took a short walk, which he had accomplished for a considerable length of time, before settling down to compose at about 9 am until he broke for lunch at about 1 pm. The remainder of the day was taken up with a long walk, tea, and cucumber sandwiches at 4 pm with his wife, perhaps followed by some more work, a deadly martini at 6 pm, and the remainder of the day was spent reading or playing a game of cards with his wife.

While the habits for productive people are fascinating, they aren't that functional or effectively pertinent to the habit you need to make. Neither of these new timetables reveals to us how Darwin thought of the hypothesis of standard determination or how Wodehouse figured out how to get Bertie Wooster into and afterward out of such a large number of engaging scratches (albeit both would have been unattainable without the work habits they'd built up). Neither does Seinfeld's efficiency tip to clarify his outstanding humor.

Productive individuals can give motivation and inspiration, yet not show a diagram for another's habits. As researchers are heard to mumble: the plural of the story isn't information! Their examples of overcoming adversity give pieces and seeds; however, they don't give the points of interest. They can enlighten us regarding the physical procedures, their timetables, and shortcomings; however, they aren't great revelers on their mental procedures.

We are left with a wide range of questions: What habit would be advisable for us to attempt to make? Where does the inspiration originate from? When and by what means would it be a good idea for you to play out the conduct, you need to turn into a habit? In what capacity would it be advisable for you to address disappointment and regular bothers?

The accompanying accounts of success in making habits are from scientific examinations. Hundreds, in some cases thousands, of individuals in these investigations have been attempting to make changes in their lives, and psychologists have estimated how fruitful they've been and made inferences about what techniques work best. From these examinations develops a progression of systems that ought to be pertinent to practically any sort of habit.

Before we see how to create another habit, we have to return at the stage to consider the inspiration. Why, precisely, would you like to make another habit? In some cases, the reasons are clear and needn't bother with any further soul-looking, yet this generally isn't the situation. Individuals regularly race into attempting to make new habits without asking themselves what the new habit will accomplish for them. There must be an ultimate objective that is worth accomplishing, or the habit will be difficult to instill. What we find in the question is that when individuals' objectives begin to debilitate, or are feeble in any case, it's hard to begin shaping another habit. A couple of moments spent considering this before you make a plunge will deliver profits over the long haul.

How about starting by offering one bit of awful guidance with a thump on the head? Numerous mainstream self-improvement guides reveal that imagining finishing your objective is gainful. The hypothesis mentions that if we can picture our future success, at that point, this will help spur us. There is some possibility that being particular about the future can be useful, yet there are entanglements.

One of the important issues is fantasizing about arriving at our objectives, which can be hazardous in it. The awful news about fantasizing was underlined by an investigation that set it in opposition to positive expectations. This examination found that members who anticipated success, as opposed to daydreaming about it, we're bound to make a move. The issue with positive dreams is that they permit us to imagine success in the present time and place. They don't make us aware of the issues we're going to encounter and can leave us with less inspiration when all things considered. It feels like we've just arrived at our objective.

Expecting success is tied in with being down to earth. We need to ponder what is exceptionally conceivable. One method for making it progressively clear what sorts of habit change are conceivable is by using perception. Instead of fantasizing a progressively powerful method for what's to come, consider the procedures that are associated with arriving at an objective, as opposed to merely the end-condition of accomplishing it.

One investigation shows that some students pictured their definitive objective of doing an admirable test or the means they would take to arrive at that objective, and the outcomes were visible. Members who imagined themselves reading and picking up the necessary information spent longer examining the test and showed signs of improvement than individuals who just pictured their objective. Imagining a result doesn't work because of the arranging of false notions. The ordinary suspicion of arriving at our objective will be a lot simpler than it truly needs to be, despite everything that strikes individuals after a long time of understanding. It may very well be hard to imagine the propensity of things when it doesn't work out as planned.

An expression of caution should be noted when picking another habit to build up. With habit change, individuals frequently attempt to take on more than they could deal with. One reaction to being discontent with ourselves is to go for a total rehash—attempt to maintain a strategic distance from this. Practically all the examinations of making new habits proffer to elementary practices, and still, very few people succeed. It's more advisable, to begin with, baby steps. If the technique works, rerun it for different habits you need to set up. On the other hand, you can reduce a more significant habit into its segment parts and work on each one independently.

The acclaimed behaviorist B. F. Skinner used this technique known as "shaping" of working up habits individually to get pigeons to play ping pong. If that doesn't dazzle you, at one point, he had a rodent responding to the "Star-Spangled Banner" by lifting a little American banner and saluting with its front leg. It's everything about layering one simple habit onto another.

Making habits, however, is about something beyond the process. Individuals will have freestyle thoughts verging on dreams about how to change themselves; while what we require for our new habits to stick. Every one of those repeated processes we have to complete won't occur without responsibility. Mental research has taken a look at the procedures which help rid of the dreams and subsequently support our odds of making permanent changes in ourselves. Two systems we may generally use to make habit change arrangements are to imagine the issues decided, and then consider why we are discontent with the present circumstance. In various manners, each might give us the inspiration we need. Yet, in reality, do they get the job done?

In some researches made by Gabriele Oettingen, New York University, these strategies were set to oppose one another. Then another system was included. As a test, members in their examination were given an issue to brood while separated into three groups. In each gathering, they were advised to use one of the three systems while taking care of the issue:

- Indulge: Imagine a positive vision of the issue explained.

- Dwell: Consider the negative parts of the present circumstance.

- Contrast: This was the new method. In the first place, members imagined a positive vision of the issue explained, then thought about the negative parts of the real world. Given both, members were approached to do a "rude awakening," contrasting their dream and reality.

The outcomes indicated that the differentiation method urged individuals to make arrangements, plans, and in making obligations when desires for progress were strong. At the point when desires for taking care of the issue were low, those in the mental complexity condition made fewer arrangements and assumed less liability. What the differentiation method had was letting individuals choose whether their objective was extremely attainable or not. At that point, if they expected to succeed, they submitted to focus on the objective; if not, they let it go. This is what we are searching for when we need to make another habit. We need to know how conceivable forming this new habit is.

This all sounds fine in principle, yet the vital issue with mental differentiating is hard. Contemplating the negative parts of our objectives is undesirable; correspondingly, uniting dream, and the truth is awkward that out of nowhere, it becomes clear what should be done, and this knowledge can be discouraging. Another point that shows the method is troublesome is how individuals detest moving from glad to be discouraging thoughts. If we feel cheerful, we need to continue pondering upbeat things, and in case we're thinking negative thoughts, it's hard to change it to positive.

The conflict between the dream of building up a habit for rehearsing the piano and the deterrents you'll face can be discouraging. When you anticipate yourself advancing, you realize it will feel brilliant to play those Bach console concertos impeccably, yet by what method will you put in the hundreds or thousands of long stretches of training required? In what capacity will you make the reality in your life away from family and work? All the more significantly: Have you purchased a piano yet? Have you confronted the truth about how you'll make the time and assurance to rehearse? However, the examination recommends you to make a move sooner, feel more empowered, and make a more noteworthy enthusiastic responsibility for building the habit.

Chapter 10
Analyze the Way you Think and Look the World

According to many psychologists, your past has a direct on your life today. We will explain how to know yourself and the various ways that your past influences your present behavior and how to handle your past presently.

How Your Past Affects Your Present

When you embark on a journey to know yourself to live a fulfilling life, you need to investigate the clutter in your past. Clutter in your past can act as the obstacles in today's life, hindering you from moving forward. Your experiences today are likely to have been influenced by your past experiences, as well. The way you act or interact with people today, maybe as a result of events in your childhood or young adulthood life. It is essential to understand the connection between your present and your past and how your past influences your future or present. All events, regardless of how big or small they were, are likely to influence your current life and your future.

Your personality and behavior today may be the result of past experiences. When a child is born, they start collecting information from their environment and end up forming beliefs based on the information they gather. Psychologists say that children can absorb information so fast that by the age of 6 years, they have formed some beliefs.

During your childhood and your teenage life, you are likely to have formed many beliefs, and these have influenced your personality and behavior today. The beliefs that you formed in your earlier life, they are likely to influence you negatively or positively. It is possible to change your negative beliefs and transform your life, although it is not easy and requires a lot of patience and discipline.

Change Your Beliefs to Change Your Personality

You may ask yourself how it is possible to change your beliefs. First, begin by acknowledging the beliefs that have molded your personality over the years. After establishing them, it is time to dig into your past and identify what leads you to form those beliefs.

This is not easy to do because as the beliefs were getting formed, you may not have been aware, hence you feel powerless over them. However, once you are able to get to the root of why you formed certain beliefs, it gets easier to deal with them. Identifying and understanding how they were formed is what gives you the power to break free from their hold. To understand it better, consider the following scene:

Suppose your boss complains that your performance was below average, and you did not deliver as expected. He says he expects better performance in the new month; will you want to know what went wrong and how it happened to fix it? The same way in your behavior, if you don't understand what caused you to behave in a certain way, then it will be impossible to change it. This is the main reason why to change and start living a better life free of negativity, identify your past influence of the mind. Know how it was formed and where it came from, and then you can deal with the clutter conclusively by transforming yourself.

Examples

These few illustrations serve to show you how your past can shape your present.

If a boy grew up in a violent household, where he saw his father abuse the mother physically, and the mother accepted it, the boy may grow to believe this to be normal behavior. When he gets married, he is likely to be abusive to his partner because it is a norm for him and does not understand why his partner does not accept it.

A child that was abused will believe that he is worthless as compared to others because of how he was treated. This child grows up with low self-esteem and is likely to become very withdrawn and live with shame all his life. In his later life, he may become shy and scared that he may be abused again.

A last-born child is likely to receive a lot of attention all around him, and as a result, he has develops a need to be always recognized. This need for attention will be with him, and when he becomes an adult, he may be very selfish and self-centered. The child may choose a career that puts him in the spotlight so that he remains the center of attention.

The above examples are just to explain how experiences in the past can cause a person to develop certain beliefs hence explaining their behavior and character in the present life. Maybe you will not be aware of why you have a certain personality or behave in a certain way. If you truly desire to change your life for better, you need a purpose to change your mind from the negative beliefs.

Psychology - Understand, Accept, Heal the Past, Understand the Present

Every person has had a past with some people having more painful pasts than others or more pleasant memories of the past. Past experiences are known to influence your present life or behavior. Most painful pasts leave people with pain because of some traumatic experience they had. Some people, even to deal with their painful memories, they opt to suppress them with the hope of forgetting the traumatic experience. They find themselves in destructive behaviors like overeating, anger issues, drinking, isolation, and many more. Healing from this is not easy; however, it is possible and doable. There are a few steps or strategies that will help you in your path, these are;

Evaluate your experiences – You must face it because you cannot deny it. Allow yourself to be open to thoughts, inner experiences, and feelings. Pick an aspect of your experience and meditate on it and notice what it makes you feel. You may notice you experience varied feelings or emotions towards it. This helps you increase your awareness of the incidence.

Be accepting and compassionate – As you meditate through your experience, try to understand it and empathize with it. This allows you to be compassionate towards yourself, and ease of your emotional challenges comes. This helps you to understand the experience, accept it happened, and forgive yourself for it.

Take a break, it is important – It is not easy to face your pains and fears; it takes great courage but moves cautiously. Pay attention to the experiences that do not rush through. When you feel overwhelmed by emotions, it is advisable to take a break; when you feel better, resume. The key thing is purposing to increase your self-awareness to a tolerable pace.

Calm yourself – To soothe yourself, learn how to mindfully breathe, focus on your breathing while blocking everything else out. You can also decide to engage in a positive activity like exercise that greatly relieves stress.

Bring it all together – This is the point where to heal past pain, you must acknowledge its existence. Recognize the pain, accept it, and be compassionate towards it. You notice you start developing a deeper self-awareness over the experience while increasing your tolerance over it. As you progress, learn to recognize when you are approaching your limit of what you can handle and calm yourself down at that point. When you keep doing this, you realize you may not change how you relate to yourself, and your pain in the past may not change, but it will change your experience allowing you to forge forward with a more positive attitude in your life.

Recognize and Break Negative Thought Patterns

When a person forms a certain habit out of routine things they do, it can become a very powerful mental tool. Recognizing and treating an individual's thought process is not easy. When you cut yourself, you can easily use an anti-bacterial cream and bandage the wound, and in no time, you are good to go.

On the contrary, with negative thoughts, it is not as easy. If the negative thoughts stem from depression, anxiety, phobias, or other mental conditions, it becomes harder to change them.

Negative thoughts are compared to paper cuts that a person keeps forming when they have no idea of what is the cause for it. Sometimes a person will not realize they have negative thoughts until they begin to affect their lives.

Depending on an individual's triggers and condition, they will need various approaches to psychotherapy, medication, and lifestyle changes. If therapy is not included as part of the treatment, it may be difficult for a person to get quick treatment.

One way a person can break from their negative thought pattern is by gradually making a mental shift. To shift how you think, it will mean you are aware of the negative thoughts, and you make a conscious decision to change them. Examine how you reflect on different situations or what you are thinking about the particular situation and switch your focus to something else. This calls for undoing negative behaviors and how one has programmed their mind through learned things. For instance, if as you were growing up, you were told that you must be the best in life and school, you may have programmed your mind for perfectionism. This can be very stressful, and making a shift mentally is a great way to fight against stress and anxiety. You must learn your most prevalent thought patterns, recognize negative thinking, and how you can redirect yourself and have constructive thoughts.

How Do you Recognize Your Negative Thoughts?

The "Should" Thoughts

When you realize your thoughts are surrounded by the word "should," you need to stop and think. For instance, thoughts like:

I should feel better, or do or act,

I should exercise daily.

I should change the way I'm eating.

I should change the way I think

The intentions behind these thoughts are noble. Based on your situation, it would be healthier to exercise and eat whole foods. The word "should," however, can cause guilty thoughts and cause you having more negative thoughts.

The ANTs

Apart from "should" thoughts, recognize other patterns that lead to automatic negative thinking. Behind the "should" statements, it is possible to have other cognitive distortions in negative thinking. These are called Automatic Negative Thoughts (ANTs).

When you have a strong reaction or feelings towards something, ANTs are your initial thoughts. They are more like reflexes rather than having freethinking. ANTs are learned and very persistent, mostly repeating themes like phobias or danger. ANTs are very common in persons with depressive or anxious thinking.

ANTs in individuals suffering from anxiety cause them to go on overdrive, turning their thoughts into serious panic attacks. Unfortunately, recognizing ANTs is not easy. Many people have had them all their lives and do not know it.

The current situation.

Your attitude or moods towards the situation.

What thoughts or image comes to mind at that moment?

Once you establish this, you must activate your thoughts into more productive ones that are wiser and helpful.

What is causing you to be Anxious?

When you start recording your thoughts, you are putting your thoughts through a test. Begin by questioning yourself on what, who, where, or when. By doing this, it helps you describe what went on while ensuring you do not deviate from the facts to feelings.

Chapter 11
The Relationship between Overthinking, Anxiety, Stress and Negative Thinking

It is fascinating to learn that our thoughts define what happens to us. From a psychological perspective, it means that we can control what happens to us by simply learning how to control our thoughts. This is a powerful technique, indeed. Knowing that you have power over what happens to you is something that most people are unaware of. The reality is that you become what you think. If you look closely, whatever happens to you, good or bad, stems from your thoughts?

What you think about affects your mental health and well-being. Your thoughts lead to the emotional state that you might be experiencing. Often, this will affect your health. If your thoughts are preoccupied with sad events, then the chances are that you will constantly feel sad. If you are constantly thinking about the fun activities that you engage in with your friends, then you attract the same energy to your life. From this, you will garner deeper insight into why your thoughts could be identified as the cause for your dwindling productivity at work, lack of sleep, and you're failing social relationships.

The Law of Attraction

If you are concerned about the direction that your life is taking, then the law of attraction may be a useful tool to get you back on track. On the surface, you might conclude that this is a law that helps you to attract things around you. Well, just as the name suggests, this is a powerful law that suggests that you attract what you focus on, believe it or not, this law is always working to shape your life. What people do not understand is that they are constantly shaping their lives consciously or subconsciously. The life that you have today is attributed to what you thought about years ago. Sure, you might not get exactly what you wanted, but you will be better off than thinking negatively.

Your future is shaped by the way you think and the way you respond to situations today. Therefore, if you think that the coming months will be difficult for you, rest assured that they are more likely to be difficult. On the other hand, if you have the perception that you are going to have fun, then you are more likely to enjoy life as it unfolds itself to your expectations.

The law of attraction is based on a simple concept. You attract what you choose to focus on. Whether you choose to think negatively or positively, it's all up to you. If you choose to focus on the positive side of life, then you will attract good things your way. You will always be full of joy and abundance; you will live your life feeling energetic and ready to handle anything that comes your way. On the contrary, if you choose to focus on the negative, your life will be full of misery; you will never be happy with the people around you. Often, you will feel as though you are tired of living. Your productivity at work and home will be negatively affected. You will always be that person that finds the negative in everything. All of this is a result of what you choose to focus on.

Knowing how the law of attraction works can unlock the doors of success in your life. This law opens your mind to the realization that we live in a world of infinite possibilities, infinite joy, and infinite abundance. Think about it. You can put your faith in your beliefs and help change future outcomes. Isn't that amazing? Unfortunately, few people understand the law of attraction and how to use it to transform their lives effectively.

Your thoughts and feelings will work together to build an ideal future for yourself. Since you have the power to decide what you want, you ought to request a life that you've always dreamt of living. Your focus and energy should be in line with what you want to attract.

How to Use the Law of Attraction

After understanding the fact that you are the creator of your own world, you should begin thinking consciously towards creating a better life for yourself. In this case, this should encourage you to think positively since your thoughts define what you want in life. This requires that you channel your time and energy on thinking about the good things you want in life. It also means that you should deliberately manage your thoughts and emotions as they have an impact on what manifests.

Ask, Believe, Receive

The law of attraction appears to be a straightforward process where you just ask for what you want, and you will receive it. However, the application process requires more than just asking and receiving. If it were this simple, then everybody would be living happy lives free of stress and anxiety. So, what is it that makes the law of attraction simple yet daunting to apply?

- **Ask**

People make requests to the universe every day, either consciously or unconsciously, through their thoughts. Whatever you think about is what you focus on. This is where you have channeled your energy. Using the law of attraction, you should realize that you must take deliberate actions to manage your thoughts and emotions. In this regard, you have to decide that you want something intentionally. This also demands that you should live and act as though you already have that which you are asking for.

- **Believe**

For you to manifest what you want in your life, it is imperative that you truly believe that you will receive what you want. Your thoughts should reflect the certainty that you have in knowing that you will get what you want. Therefore, your mind should be free of doubts. This is the trickiest part of the law of attraction.

Most people simply ask. However, they find it difficult to believe that they can get what they want. The aspect of belief diminishes when individuals realize that what they asked for is taking longer to manifest than they expect. So, they turn their attention to negative thinking. They begin to convince themselves that it is impossible. Life is not easy. Such perceptions only affect what you are asking for from the universe. The worst thing is that negativity bias begins to take shape. Without realizing, they attract negativity in their lives because they simply failed to believe.

- **Receive**

The last thing that you need to do is to receive what you were asking or hoping for. Perhaps this is the easiest part, since it only requires you to position yourself in the best way through your emotions to receive your gift. Consider an ordinary situation where you are receiving a gift from your loved ones. Certainly, you express from your body language that you are happy. Emotions of love and appreciation should be evident when receiving any gift. This is how the universe expects you to receive your reward.

You should live your day feeling thankful and happy for what you already have. This is the best way in which you can practice receiving what you want even before the world gives it to you. These emotions can also be shaped by how you choose to think. Accordingly, it is recommended that you should live mindfully by enhancing your self-awareness, to stop yourself each time negative thoughts develop in your mind.

At first, it won't be an easy feat to control your thoughts and emotions. Nevertheless, it is worth noting that everything good calls for patience and practice. As such, for the law of attraction to work for you, you have to be patient. You have to keep practicing the habit of believing. Most importantly, always remember that you can create your happiness.

Anxiety; Stopping Negative Thoughts

Anxiety is caused by numerous factors. At times, it is caused by a combination of genetic factors and environmental factors. The fear within you can easily make you feel worried about things that haven't happened. In extreme cases, this leads to panic. Your mind can easily amplify the fears within you and make you believe that something bad will happen. In social settings, anxiety will leave you in a constant state of worry of saying the wrong thing in front of other people. Also, you might gain the assumption that other people will not like you. Such negative thoughts only prevent you from being yourself. It holds you back from living your life.

Common Thoughts in Anxious People

There are certain stressful thoughts evident in anxious people. Below are a few examples of some of these thoughts. Identifying these thoughts is helpful as it ensures that you find a way to deal with your anxiety. Examples of common thoughts in anxious people are as follows.

- "I am not good at what I do."

Anxious individuals will focus more on the negative aspects of themselves. In any setting, their minds will constantly think about their weaknesses. It will be difficult for them to reflect on their strengths and why they were chosen for a particular role in their place of work. Anxiety will make you feel as though your boss will fire you anytime, for example.

- "I am going to forget."

Have you ever felt that you were going to forget something even before the actual thing occurred? This is a sign that you are anxious. Believing that you are going to forget something simply means that you can't trust yourself. You're raising doubts in your mind that you can't remember to do something either during the day, tomorrow, or soon.

- "Nobody likes me."

In the social media world, it is very easy for an anxious person to conclude that people don't value them because they are not getting any responses to their posts. This trait portrays someone who thinks too much. This is a person who is always worried about what other people might say. As a result, they will be too concerned about their social media posts and the responses they will be getting.

- "What if I am next?"

Without a doubt, we live in a world of uncertainty. You can never be sure about tomorrow. This can have an impact on your attitude towards the unknown. There are times when you might be scared that the worst could happen to you at any time. Concerning this, you should understand that it is common to experience such thoughts. However, this doesn't mean that you should allow such thoughts to overwhelm you. Since you have some level of control of your thoughts, you should learn how to manage them. Living in constant worry that you might stumble any minute is no way to live.

- "My partner hasn't called, they must be mad at me."

Anxiety can also affect your relationships in many ways. Consider an ordinary example where your partner fails to call you during the day. There are many reasons why this could have happened. Maybe they were busy, or their phone was out of battery. However, your worrying nature will give you the assumption that your partner is upset at you for some reason. Having this perception will only ruin the beautiful relationship you share with your partner.

- "Did I leave the door open?"

Most people will worry too much about the simple things that they might have forgotten to do. For instance, you might question yourself about your door, appliances, or your light switches. You will find your mind wandering, thinking about whether or not the appliances were switched off. Doing this repeatedly will only lead to anxiety.

Chapter 12
How to Manage Your Time Efficiently?

Why Can You not Manage Your Time Efficiently?

Managing your time effectively is an important part of self-discipline. If you are unable to manage your time properly, you will not be able to accomplish the goals that you wish to complete in life and work. Time management is something that most people are taught in school. However, it is often not taught to them efficiently, and those that fail can contribute their failure to a lack of time management. By putting pleasure above workload, you are creating an imbalance with your time management strategy. This means that you are using the instant gratification as your driving force instead of the long-term gratification. Those that are in balance will experience greater happiness, less stress, and more financial freedom.

Time management is the act of prioritizing the tasks that you must do on a schedule that is specific and calculated. Several mistakes are made by those that fail at time management. Each one of these mistakes is listed below with details on how it will affect your life. I have also included ways to combat these failures.

1 Mistake: Not maintaining a list of to-dos

There are many times that I would stare off into space, and my kids would ask me what is wrong. Only for me to reply to, "I feel like I forgot something." Have you ever experienced this? If so, then you will understand what I mean about the value of a well thought out to-do list. The to-do list helps to organize the day. It provides a schedule of events and a timeline of what one needs to accomplish today, this week, and this month. Without a to-do list, one would have this conversation with their kids daily. If you are experiencing moments of forgetfulness, then you should invest in the time it takes to make a to-do list.

When you do not use your to-do list to accomplish your goals, you place yourself at risk of failure as well as disappointment. The most effective way to use a to-do list is to prioritize the things that are on your list. This can be done in several different ways.

The a-f process:

By labeling your high priority items with an A and your low priority items with an F, you can begin to categorize the tasks that you need to do.

For instance, say you need to buy groceries, call your mom, and schedule a Dr. Appt.

You would need to label these in this order:

- A=Schedule Appt.

- B=Call Mom.

- C=Buy Groceries.

Bullet points to-do process:

With the bullet point process, you will have a key that will tell you what items need to be purchased, what items are to-dos, what appointments need to be scheduled, as well as attended, which items have been completed, and which items have been moved to another day.

Your key can look similar to this one:

- To show a to-do list item.

- To show an appointment that is scheduled.

- To show that something has been completed.

- To show that something has been moved to another day.

You do not have to use these symbols. You can use anything that you would like to use. I use squares for my to-dos, a line through each task to show completion, an arrow through each task to show I have moved it to another day, and a circle to show an appointment. This helps to keep track of things in a way that makes it interesting as well as useful.

If you are dealing with simple projects, you can be super vague; however, if you are dealing with a complex project, you will need to use bullet points and indentations to show the individual tasks that need to be completed for the result.

By breaking down all the things you need to do into smaller, much simpler tasks, you can have a less overwhelming time management tool.

An example of this would be to write down the steps that it would take to write your first novel. However, this can seem huge. So instead, underneath this title, you will need to write down things like:

- Designate the set characters.

- Chose the location.

- Chose the theme.

- Decide on the plot for each character.

- Decide on the title for the.

- Research the culture of the characters, the background, the language, the behaviors, and mannerisms.

- Build an outline that encompasses all things into it.

- Build a synopsis that will explain the storyline.

These are just a few of the steps that you would need to break down into much smaller steps. This will give you a less overwhelming and more accurate idea of what is necessary for the writing of a novel.

2 Mistake: Personal goals have not been set

Your personal goals pertain to the goals that are specific to your needs and your desires for the future. So, what is it that you want to do in the next year? What about the next five years? You can take this even further and determine what you want to do in the next ten years. This will help you to schedule your time wisely so that you can begin to build upon your goals.

This is an essential part of managing your time and building a foundation for your future. To reach your destination, you will need to have a vision of what you want. This vision will help you to make small achievable steps to accomplish all the things that need to be done to get you to the result. This helps with the management of resources as well as priorities that are necessary for a proper SMART goal.

These will also help us to determine the most important tasks that need to be done first, as well as the things that you need to avoid so that you do not have distractions.

SMART goals are goals that are:

- *Specific.*
- *Measurable.*
- *Accountable.*
- *Realistic.*
- *Trackable.*

By setting goals for each one of these categories, you will be able to build a foundation for discipline and goal setting that is sustainable.

3 Mistake: Not scheduling your tasks by priority

It is extremely hard to understand prioritizing the tasks that you have properly and functionally. If you are currently working on an important task, then you need to stay focused and not allow distractions to interfere with your train of thought. This means if something comes up, that is not life or death, then stay focused and determined not to be sidetracked. Then when you are done, you will be able to handle the situation that arose while working. This allows you to show priority to the things that are most important at that time.

In those moments, when you find your secretary or assistant presenting you with another task to complete, you should inform them that you are in the middle of a task already and will place this one on the list in the proper priority category. If your children interrupt your train of thought while working on something important, then simply ask them to wait their turn. This is a simple way of showing priority over a situation that seems dire but is not. False emergencies will arise throughout your day; the key is to prioritize properly so that you do not allow distractions to interfere with your workday progress. Not all things will need to be immediately started or accomplished; some things can be put off until a better time presents itself. So, consider what the most important task is and finish that before being distracted by other less important things.

By prioritizing the tasks that you need to do, you are learning how to manage your time efficiently. This can lead to a more concise and steadier schedule. Determining what is most important for completion within your workday is crucial to accomplishing the tasks at hand. Place those things that are most important within prominent spots on your schedule and, at times, that you are most alert and energized. This will ensure that you have completed the important work first, and then you can tackle the other work in a systematic order.

4 Mistake: Distractions are interfering with your focus, and you fail to manage them appropriately

It is scientifically proven that you will lose at least 2 hours out of every day due to unwanted distractions. Consider how much time you are losing on your day and determine if you are wasting more time than you are using properly. Are you distracted easily? Do you find that others interrupt your focus regularly? Is there something that you can do to avoid being distracted?

Distractions are an inevitable part of work. When you work in an environment that involves several co-workers, then you will be faced with the distractions that stem from interruptions, meetings being called, and sometimes tedious and pointless social interactions with others. These things can be avoided if you have a private office where you can close the door and limit the interaction with others. By placing a closed-door policy at your office, you can instill some boundaries and guidelines that will help you to avoid distractions from others. Inform your office staff that if the door is closed, then you are not to be disturbed. This sets a precedent on when and how they can approach you for questions and complications as well as any other distracting interactions. However, make sure that you do not keep the door closed all day since they will need your guidance throughout the day. For your workday to run smoothly, you will need to have the channels of communication open and running smoothly. However, setting a time of the day that you need to be left alone is optimal for continued focus on your workday without distractions.

Another way to avoid distractions is to be fully in the moment. For instance, do not handle emails and work-related stuff during dinner with the family. You also do not want to handle family-related stuff during your workday. This will place you at the right time, right place mentally. Do not allow emails, IM's, phone calls, or other distracting communication to interfere in your mealtime with family. You also do not want to be interrupted when dealing with work-related times or those times that you are super focused on the task at hand. Find a balance between personal and work hours.

You need to have a proper balance and flow when it comes to your schedule. To balance your schedule, you need to determine what is most important for that day. When you can be 100 percent in your current task, then you will be able to provide more focus to that task, which makes completion effortless. By not allowing distractions in your workday, you are allowing yourself to be focused on completing the work you are assigned promptly. By minimizing distractions, you can gain the control you need to work through the day and complete the best work that you can for that specific project.

There are a few things that you can do to avoid distractions:

- Turn off your instant messaging options on the computer.
- Turn the sound off on your phone.
- Shut down all social media notifications.
- Shut your door and inform co-workers that you are busy with work.

Chapter 13
Start, Do, Achieve

In the success of every successful person, there is a journey to be walked on, and there is always a start, middle, and end phase of it. Every phase contains the things that you should do at your best so that you can finally accomplish the achievement that you desire and target from the beginning.

Looking at this perspective, in this, I try to see what are the activities that can be done to support your effort. For this, I separated each of the tips into the three phases that you have to go through to get your success in the end eventually. I call it **Start**, **Do**, and **Achieve** phases and insert the tips in each of them so you can optimize your effort in them.

At the start of things, when you finally decide to begin to work on the things you love, for sure, seriously, you have to layout things and plan how you are going to take on the effort to achieve your success. The goal for your effort and the formulation of how to get there and realize it is some things that have to be taken care of in this phase. The only thing that you can be sure where you want to head in terms of working based on your passion continuously and get the general direction and guidance so you can be better prepared to achieve it.

Then, when you finally walk and implement the plan that you have formulated, you will see and understand more of the things in your passion area as they are in the situation that surrounds you during your effort and you must choose how to react to it, evaluate and put the necessary effort consistently, and keep developing yourself to become a better person who is more ready to realize the success that you want.

Thus, eventually, you will get your success if you have put in enough effort always. From there, what do you want to do, so you can cultivate the knowledge and skills that you have already got that passion of yours and become the person who can bring a significant positive impact to that? The choice is, of course, entirely yours to act in the way that becomes the benefit to a lot of people around you, in the community, and the society as a whole once you reach the top. You shall see how your expertise of things can help you more in doing that.

And based on that understanding for each phase of success journey for your working passion, here is a brief explanation of activities in each phase of achieving success in it.

Define Your Passion Success (Start): The most important thing when you start your journey is to know where you will go to. Thus, you will begin your work by deciding the things you want to achieve in your work. It has to be strong why for you so you can always remember it as the reason for you to keep on working hard and maintain the determination that you have.

Plan Your Way (Start): After you have defined the things that you want to target while working on the things that you love, then you should plan how to get there. What is the timeframe, and what are the activities that you need to do in general to get you closer and closer to your targets? Think about it before you begin to put in the effort.

Take the Daily Steps (Do): Success always consists of small steps that are taken day by day, time after time, before you ultimately reach that destination. Thus, it is important to remember to take a persistent effort in doing your passion so you can reach your targets in it. In this, we will try to see the things that you must pay attention to during your hard work so you can be more efficient, effective, and productive while doing that required work for success.

Dive Into the Area Network (Do): It is always better to know and engage with the people that have the same interest with you in your work, especially if it is something like working on the things that you are passionate about. It can stimulate your effort and bring you the opportunities that bring you closer to your goals, which might not be discovered if you just work on yourself. We will take a look at what you can do to optimize yourself in your passion area network.

Learn and Be Better (Do): There is always something to learn from for each person, and there are always some ways that you can develop yourself in the work that you love. By giving way to improve your knowledge, skill, and attitude about your passion, then you can enhance the productivity of your work and know more efficient and effective ways to get the job done. What are the ways that you can do that to improve yourself?

Keep the Perseverance and Determination in Passion (Do): There are always struggles and problems that can prevent you from achieving success, even when you do the things that you are passionate about. Events like failures, rejections, or doubts from other people are the things that seem to occur to everyone on their road to success. For that, you must develop the perseverance and determination so you can keep going forward.

Attain and Improve Your Passion Success (Achieve): You have accomplished the achievements that you want, but the hard work does not stop there. You have to put in the effort to maintain or even have the desire to achieve more goals after this to keep on having the motivation for the work in your passion. Understand how you can still be inspired for more success, even after you have realized your original goals.

Enlarge the Scope (Achieve): Now that you have begun to enjoy the fruits of your labor from doing the things that you love and know how to maintain and improve on it, what is more there that you can do? Well, you can empower your passion area using the expertise that you have already got! Find out how you can do that and enhance the way that you can apply the specific knowledge and skills that you have already got to contribute positively to the people around you.

Give Back to the Community (Achieve): After you have got to the top of things in your area, there is much that you can give to the group that you grow in during the journey to the success that you have and contribute to the communities which have the relevancy to the expertise that you have. We will take a look deeper into how you can focus your effort on that optimally, so that you and the community members can benefit from it.

There are probably more general and specific things that can be explored about your specific passion for improving the chance of success in working your passion for living, and you can definitely do that also to the things listed above. However, if you are disciplined in doing the right things when you work on each of the phases and keep on trying to improve yourself in the area that you love consistently, then you should get the most from the hard work that you do to reach to the top in the respective area of your passion.

The journey to success is definitely long, whatever the area that you work in or the passion that you have. It has its ups and downs, and it will take the very best of you to navigate your way to achieve things that have a huge meaning for you in life. Every person has a different journey and a different passion. It is up to each person, including you, to keep putting in the effort so he/she can get the achievement desired on the things that he/she loves.

So, with that in mind, let's take a look at each phase's tip and keep on working hard on your way to success in the work that you love!

Define your Passion Success

What do you want to achieve in the area that you love? What do you define as your ultimate success when trying to make your passion as something that you work every day for a living?

Well, you should think about it as soon as you decide to start trying to make your hobby something that you can accomplish your life achievement from. After all, no journey is worth it to be taken without a clear destination of where you go to.

I mean, try to think about it. If you want to go somewhere, but you don't know where your destination is, then what is the point of going at all? What is the motivation that you should have and where you should point your hard work if you say that you don't know the objective of the things that you do?

Hence, you must always begin things with the end. Try to connect the work that you will do according to your passion to that after you have defined the goals that you want and the things that you consider as success in them.

And it must be a strong goal too, a strong why for your hard work that you can refer back to time and time again when you face a struggle during your journey to success. If you don't have a powerful reason why you want to do the things that you do and why you want to take the work of your passion seriously, then you most probably will quit after few hurdles that you will face and doubt the commitment need of your daily effort.

So, take your time and formulate something that you think is important to you so that you want to take on this road to success. Because it can be frustratingly long and take a lot of labor from you to navigate your way through.

Try to focus on some goals too that you want to achieve while working on the things that you love. Having something such as 20 goals that you want to accomplish is surely great if you can accomplish them all. However, it will surely take a much longer time and break your focus significantly when you need it the most in your effort. Therefore, try to narrow it down to 3-5 goals that you think are the most important things to achieve in your life. That way, you can have the understanding on what you want, center your effort to them, while also having more possibility to form the strong goals that are mentioned earlier as the things you can hold into when things get tough.

However, you probably have a hard time when thinking about what things should be your end goals when you work on the things that you love? Here are three tips from me that you can take a look into and do to help you define them.

Chapter 14
Coping with Depression

Depression is a severe psychiatric problem that is often developed from anxiety and fear. It causes feelings of hopelessness and despair that often interferes with the ability to do everyday tasks. Some people face a single interaction with depression at a certain point in life, while others experience depression as an ongoing lifetime issue.

Some symptoms that may suggest that you have depression include social withdrawal, intense mood swings, poor sleep, fatigue, and thoughts of suicide. Psychotic depression is also a major issue that can cause hallucinations and delusions. These symptoms are usually caused by depression, reflecting and magnifying feelings of despair and negative emotions instead of being caused by a significant brain disorder.

When you suffer from depression over long periods, then you may have dysthymia. Dysthymia is a form of chronic depression that causes feelings of unhappiness but usually doesn't affect a person's ability to function normally. There's also seasonal affective disorder, which affects an individual at the same time each year, normally when the seasons change. A major depressive disorder is your standard level of depression that doesn't normally occur at a set point in life but causes either a single incident of depression or a series of depressive bouts.

Depression is very complicated, and they're usually isn't just one event that causes someone to develop depression. It's a cause of biological, environmental, and emotional factors that may occur after a significant event just as likely as it occurs seemingly at random. Just because there is no "apparent" reason to develop depression doesn't mean that you can't develop it at some point in your life.

Your standard treatment for depression includes taking antidepressant medications. Some people also take other drugs such as antipsychotic medications to fight their depression. Luckily, if you are averse to seeking out medication for your natural body response to an environmental, biological, and emotional stimulus, then there are other alternatives for you.

You can do things such as change your diet, exercise more, meditate, create meaningful relationships, and challenge your own thoughts. Here are three helpful lessons that you should include in your life whenever you feel an onset of depression so that you can change your mind and enjoy life.

Lesson 1: Experience your environment

It's not easy to feel up to doing anything when you're depressed. As much as you want just to lock yourself in your room, this often doesn't work because you'll likely stay in your head during this time. Sometimes a change of environment is all that you need to experience to feel better emotionally. Exercise is one way that you can start coping with your depression. It doesn't have to involve going to a gym every day if that's not your thing. You can simply go for a walk to the park, go for a bike ride, or jog around your neighborhood. Studies have shown that exercise is just as powerful as medication when it comes to dealing with depression. It will also help you sleep easier through the night and increase your energy levels altogether.

The recommended amount of daily exercise for most people is 30 minutes a day. That doesn't mean you have to jump right into doing a rigorous exercise right away. Start small and build your way up. Attend classes where you move your body if you enjoy doing yoga or even martial arts. Go swimming, play tennis, or just participate in an activity that makes you feel happy. That's the key to sticking with exercise in the long run.

You also don't have to exercise for thirty minutes straight. When you're feeling low, go for a walk for five to 10 minutes. This should help you feel better for at least a couple of hours. If your negative emotions or thoughts come back, all you have to do is go for another walk and notice how much better you feel. Put on your favorite music, exercise with a friend, or enjoy the company of your favorite animal, and what might be difficult to do at first will become a fun activity for all.

Lesson 2: Question your thinking

Everything that you go through while you're depressed might naturally seem negative. You might ask, "Why me?" or "why am I always put in these horrible situations?" Although these might occur naturally, you should consider your life and the situations that you find yourself in to discover if you can be optimistic or neutral about the things that happen around you.

For every negative thought that pops into your head, try and come up with a reason to see the situation in a positive light. Start by thinking outside of yourself. If the events that caused you to think negatively happened to someone else, would you still hold the same point of view? Maybe you would, but it's also possible that you can find a silver lining in the events that take place when you look at it from an outsider's perspective.

If you're the cause of your negative emotion, then maybe you're holding yourself to a standard that's too high. Many depressed people consider themselves perfectionists and don't like to disappoint themselves or others. When your life isn't exactly where you want it to be, instead of going deeper into depression, be less hard on yourself, and consider all of the wonderful attributes that you have.

Don't forget to socialize with the right people. Ask them how they would feel in your situation. Consider what they say and ask for feedback as to what they would do in that situation as well. Perhaps they can give you the perspective that you need to get over your depressed emotions. Try to be as optimistic as possible when you speak to people that are your emotional support, pick well the people who you discuss your problems with, and take their suggestions to heart. They might just offer an overlooked solution that helps you get out of your rut.

Lesson 3: Do the things that you love to do

When you ignore your true feelings and lose track of what makes you happy, then it's easy to fall into depression. Start filling your time with people and activities that bring you enjoyment. Also, make sure that you take care of your body well by watching what you eat, getting an adequate amount of sleep, and enjoying the sunlight a little bit each day.

One thing that helps a lot of people with depression has a pet. You can't replace a human connection with anything else, but having companionship can help you feel more connected to others. It also allows you to spend more time outside and boosts the amount of joy that you have for life.

Hopefully, these simple tips will help you cope with depression. They're easy to include on your daily routine for a reason, and you can use these techniques whenever you're motivated to. Simply getting in touch with your passions by watching a funny movie, reading a good book, or taking a nice relaxing bath is often enough to change your mood for the better, so that you can get back to your normal life.

Lesson 4: Outdoing Anger

Anger is another emotion that people naturally feel in reaction to the environment and situations around them. It causes physiological and biological changes in the body by triggering a fight or flight response, much like anxiety, but instead of causing fear or worry, it results in irritation, rage, and fury. Internal and external events can cause anger, so it's important to identify the cause of any anger you experience. The main way that an individual reacts to anger is through aggression. This is natural because your situation might call for a sudden response to protect yourself or your loved ones. The healthy way to deal with anger is through being assertive instead of aggressive so that you can fix the situation you find yourself without harming yourself or others. Being assertive allows you to solve your issues while being respectful and doesn't call for attacking or demanding something from another individual. That doesn't mean that you should try to hold on to or suppress your anger, but rather that you should find a new way to deal with your constructive problems.

When you hold in your anger, you're more likely to get upset with yourself, which brings about many biological and physiological issues to your body. It can also cause you to act in a non-constructive way that's passive-aggressive, cynical, or hostile. People who don't learn to control their anger in a positive way end up destroying their relationships and themselves. That's why it's important to calm down, look at your internal responses, deal with the issue appropriately, and let the feelings subside.

Managing your anger can be difficult, but it isn't impossible. Participating in anger management allows you to reduce the physical and emotional response that your body goes through on time when it counts. It's important to understand that you can't always change the people who are around you or avoid the things that make you upset, but you can control your own actions when something comes up.

Unlike with many mental illnesses, you don't need other people to tell you when you have an anger issue. You probably have already realized it yourself. That's the first step to controlling it positively. All people have different temperaments and become angry at different things and show their anger differently. Some people are naturally hotheaded when a negative event occurs, while others might show their anger by being grumpy or irritable. If you withdrawal socially or become physically ill when you're upset, this can be just as detrimental as lashing out at others or making your anger apparent. These three lessons will help you cope with your anger.

Lesson 5: Try to relax

This is especially important if you're in a relationship with another person who also has a hot temper. Cultivating relaxation in stressful situations takes time to develop, but with enough practice, you'll be able to do it. Find something that helps you relax and return to it whenever you notice yourself becoming upset. Some simple things that you can try include:

Breathing deeply and letting your body relax before deciding on an appropriate response.

Thinking calmly by reminding yourself to relax, or even counting to ten is the best basic concept to feel better. You can repeat this process as much as needed at the moment to calm down.

Make calm movements. Learning yoga or meditation can help you calm your mood and make good choices whenever you find yourself upset.

Lesson 6: Learn to communicate

Disputes normally erupt when one party doesn't understand or misunderstands what another person is suggested. Make sure that you get a full picture of something before you jump to a conclusion and act. Slow down, think about what the other people that have created the conflict are saying, and discover a way to resolve the issue without becoming enraged. Take your time before responding to someone who has upset you and acts easily.

Chapter 15
The Tools You Need

To draw on the power of positive thinking in your life, you would do better to use some tools. Here are a few methods that will cement positive thinking as an everyday habit for you, which in turn will help you fulfill your life's goals, to dream, and to find happiness.

Thoughts: What Are You Thinking?

We have seen earlier how important it is what we think. When you "talk" to yourself in your mind following a failure or any mishap, you are drawing a picture of yourself in your mind. That image imprints in your mind and stays there for a very long time. If that picture is negative, everything you do afterward will be negative.

It is important, therefore, to be careful about what thoughts you allow to dwell. You need to focus on the positive aspects of any given situation, and in those situations where you find it very hard to find anything positive at all, make an effort not to end up blaming yourself.

People with low self-esteem tend to blame themselves for everything that goes wrong around them, even those things where they had nothing to do with it. For example, they would say, "This happened because I am so unlucky." Or "This happened because wherever I go, I bring disaster."

Focus on the positive aspect of any situation. Also, teach yourself to catch those negative thoughts right in the formative period. You may not be able to help thinking, "Boy! I messed up big time!" but you can stop this thought from developing into, "I am so utterly hopeless and good-for-nothing!"

Learn to be quick in forgiving yourself and moving forward. If you have difficulty in doing that, just imagine yourself as a friend. How would you have reacted if that friend committed the mistake/ faux pas/ problem you did? It is often very easy to forgive a friend's mistake and also easy to convince the friend to "forget all about it."

Apply the same rules to yourself. Let go of the guilt and blame; learn the lesson, and move on. Encourage positive thought through your mind and believe in yourself. Be your own best friend!

Attitude: Challenge Your Thoughts

You need a positive attitude to sustain positive thoughts long enough to benefit from their power. If you have a defeatist attitude, you will end up defeated. You need to focus on developing a positive attitude and sustain it. You need to believe in yourself, be confident that you can face any type of situation, and find solutions to any problem that comes your way.

Changing your attitude is easy as long as you keep a close watch on your thoughts and do not let them get away into the negativity. You can change your attitude in 3 quick steps:

1. **Find what you need to change** – It is very important that you first identify which traits are holding you down. The exercise you did earlier to identify who you are would come in handy now. Identify one (or more) negative traits that influence your attitude and target it for a change. Attempt to make one change at a time.

2. **Find a role model to make it easier to visualize** – To make things easier, identifying a role model whom you would like to emulate. This would make it easier for you to visualize the changes you want to see in yourself.

3. **Visualize the result of the change** – See in your mind's eye how this change in attitude can change your life. What does the change mean to you? Success? Better understanding among friends? A loving relationship with your spouse or children? – And so on. Project that image as vividly as you can because the clearer the image, the easier it will be for you to transition to that change.

Belief: Boost the Strength of Your Mind

Nothing works without belief. You have to believe it can happen before you see it happen. You also have to develop a set of beliefs that support a positive attitude and promote positive thinking. Run through the following beliefs and work them into your life steadily yet firmly to ensure that you stay positive even when things don't look so good at first sight.

1. **It does not matter what people say about me** – The moment you pay attention to what others say about you, you give them control over you. Do not bother about who says and what they say. They are entitled to their opinion; also, how many people can you please, even if you tried? Best is to keep doing what you feel is right and ignore anything and anyone who thinks otherwise.

2. **I have the freedom to be me** – You should not need to put on a façade in front of your friends, loved ones, workmates, etc. You need to be yourself – the original person, nothing else. The moment you imitate anyone, you are saying loud and clear, "I am not comfortable with being myself."

3. **Life sucks sometimes, but I can do a lot of good out of what I have** – This is important because life indeed will kick plenty of dirt in your face. Instead of sitting there and crying in pain, the best way is to take cover and think of how to overcome it. Never ask, "Why me?" because bad things do also happen to good people, it's just that they handle differently. Hence, it may happen to you, too. At that time, pray that you have it in you to see the brighter side and move.

4. **I'm down today, and that is okay** – There will be times when things do not go the way you planned. Life is not always a bed of roses; sometimes, you get more thorns than flowers. At such times, you need to keep in mind that "these things happen" and will pass.

5. **I'm grateful for all I have** – Very often, when we encounter obstacles in our lives, we focus on the "have not's" instead of being grateful for what we have. It is extremely important that every day, you count the blessings you have one by one. This is especially important when you are going through hardship because it will deflect your pain and put things in a better perspective.

6. **I made a mistake. It's ok. I'm learning**. Don't kill yourself over the mistakes you make. Use the lesson and move on. Every wrong turn leads somewhere – perhaps not always the best way, but nevertheless a new way, and there is something to learn from every mistake.

7. **Things change; it's ok**. The only change is permanent. Expect everything to change. Nothing lasts forever – good or bad; things will change. Sometimes, things take a turn for the better and sometimes for worse. You need to be prepared for change and face it head-on. The more you run away from change or resist it, the harder it will be for you to be happy.

8. **My happiness comes from inside**. Your happiness does not depend upon ANYTHING external. It's on you. It is the way you love and respect yourself. It is the way you allow anything external to affect you. It is NOT coming from money, love, friends, acceptance, and professional success. It comes from inside. It comes from believing that you are special, that you deserve the best, and will get the best. Nobody should be allowed to control your happiness; that is your prerogative.

9. **I choose to stay around people who appreciate me**. Make it a point to surround yourself with people who appreciate you for what you

are. Remove yourself from people who put you down, who make you feel bad about yourself, who limit your dreams, which weigh you down. Get away from any negative influence because it will drain your positivity about life. You are the company you keep.

10. **If I'm asking whether it's worth it, it is not**. Listen to your gut feelings, especially in matters of love. If you find yourself asking, "Is this worth it?" it is NOT; because when it is, you will know 100% that it is. There is no scope of the doubt when you are in that special relationship. You know. When the question comes up, it is because there are things that need you to compromise. Don't! Don't compromise on anything that gives you happiness! Laugh at your mistakes, allow yourself to break the rules, live your life in full – you have only today; you never know what tomorrow brings.

11. **I am making a difference**. Do something good for someone. Make a difference in somebody's life. Be the answer to someone's prayers. It is hugely liberating and joyous to know that you can make a difference – for the better – in someone's life. Make it a point to do at least ONE good deed every day, big or small. You will find that your life feels blessed.

12. **I have no expectations, and I am never disappointed**. This is perhaps the most important rule of life. No matter what you do – at work, in your personal relationships, clandestine help – NEVER expect anything. The moment you expect anything, you are open to disappointment because, more often than not, you will not get what you expect. The best way is never to expect anything; hence, anything that

does come to you becomes a bonus to be celebrated. Unfulfilled expectations can make you bitter and resentful – and rob you of your happiness. Don't allow that to happen.

Will Power: This, I'll Change!

You have the will power to change what you do not like. Many times we compromise with life because we are too tired to struggle anymore. Don't. Do not stop until you get what you want out of your life. You owe yourself that much.

This little story will help you understand better. There was this person – Jeremy - who was kind, hardworking, and helpful. He got a lousy job, which was paying much less than he deserved and worked him into the ground. It was difficult for him to leave because he had a family to support, and the market was not too good for looking for another job.

Eric and Mark were Jeremy's closest friends. One day Mark was out of the way angry about Jeremy being stuck in a bad paying job and all. Eric replied, "You get what you deserve. Don't worry about that." Mark was shocked. He knew that Eric loved Jeremy; they were childhood friends. So, how could he make such a remark?

Eric explained, "See, life hands you ups and downs. Sometimes, you just have to stay down for a while. But if you are good, and you know what you want and what you are worth, you will not rest until you get what you deserve." In other words, until you think you got all that you are worth, you will keep struggling to get more. You stop only when you think it is enough.

The knowledge that you deserve better than you have today will give you the strength and will power to fight your way through to reach your goal. Hence, you should never feel too bad because you are stuck in a bad relationship, bad job, bad choice of career – make the best of what you have and move forward towards your goal.

The lesson here is that you need to be truthful to yourself about what you want out of your life and what you deserve. Do not compromise on your happiness. Have the will power to change and keep changing until you get what you deserve – and more.

Next time you find yourself stuck in any type of situation that you do not like, say to yourself firmly, "This, I will change!"

Chapter 16
Realigning Your Confidence Levels with Your Abilities

Sometimes, our confidence levels move out of alignment with our abilities, knowledge, and readiness to adapt to changing conditions. When this happens, you must evaluate ourselves and realign our confidence levels with reality.

If we're overconfident, we might be inclined to take excessive risks, dismiss others' opinions, and ignore our weaknesses. When we confront setbacks and challenges with this frame of mind, we risk being unprepared regardless of our courage.

If we're under-confident, we may avoid taking risks, allow others' opinions to control us, and perceive our weaknesses as a harbinger of certain defeat. With *this* frame of mind, we'll be hesitant to respond to setbacks and challenges altogether.

It's difficult to be mentally strong when our confidence levels are unrealistic. Both arrogance and unjustified self-doubt are the enemies of cognitive resilience and resolve. Arrogance might sustain us in the short term but will lead us off course over the long run. Unjustified self-doubt may prevent us from responding to adversity altogether, fearful of certain defeat.

Given the potential pitfalls of harboring unrealistic confidence levels, it's important to perform a periodic self-assessment. Ask yourself:

- "Are my confidence levels reasonable given my circumstances?"
- "How do I respond to criticism?"
- "Am I immediately inclined to back down when challenged?"
- "Am I eager or reluctant to share my thoughts with others?"
- "When I encounter setbacks, do I instinctively feel fearful and nervous? Or do I feel self-assured? Why?"

This self-appraisal will help you to identify whether your confidence levels need to be realigned quickly. It may also reveal areas in your life that need attention - for example, whether you react to others' criticism in a healthy, sensible manner.

Five Core Building Blocks of Self-Confidence

Improving self-confidence warrants its own. But there are several elements we can focus on today that'll boost our confidence levels with minimal effort. Most of them involve our mindset. If we embrace them and incorporate them into our day, they'll have a considerable positive impact on our self-trust.

1 - Willingness to leave your comfort zone.

By leaving our comfort zone, we expose ourselves to unfamiliar situations. Doing so reveals that such situations rarely warrant fear. On the contrary, they offer opportunities to grow, both personally and professionally. They give us a chance to surrender our need to control our circumstances and learn to adapt to new ones.

2 - Openness to experiencing emotional discomfort.

Self-confidence requires an awareness of our emotions. But it also requires that we build a tolerance to them. The only way to do so is to expose ourselves to the discomfort that accompanies negative emotions.

Many of us tend to suppress emotional pain. But we should remain open to experiencing it as doing so helps us to build resistance to it. This resistance will allow us to remain attuned to negative emotions without being paralyzed by them.

3 - Habit of self-assessment.

There's considerable value in performing self-evaluations regularly. Earlier, we talked about doing them to realign our confidence levels with reality. Here, we're broadening the scope.

It's important to sit down periodically and reflect on how you've grown. Consider the new skills you've learned. Think about particular situations in which you found yourself and how you handled them. Take stock of acquaintances you've recently met, recent conversations you've had with strangers, and tasks you performed that were once unfamiliar to you.

We're constantly growing in one way or another. This is especially the case when we leave our comfort zone (see one above). The problem is, we often fail to recognize this growth because it happens so gradually.

4 - Embrace positivity.

Maintaining a positive attitude entails suppressing negative self-talk. It involves highlighting our strengths and celebrating our successes while perceiving our weaknesses and blunders as opportunities to learn and grow.

Sadly, many of us learn to be pessimistic about ourselves, thanks to the setbacks and disappointments we experience throughout our lives. This attitude not only hampers our confidence but also prevents us from growing. The good news is, we can recondition our minds to embrace optimism and positive thinking. In doing so, we can train ourselves to recognize our ability to overcome adversity instinctively.

5 - Abandon your desire for external validation.

Seeking approval from others hurts your self-confidence. It trains your mind to distrust your motivations and abilities. Instead, your mind learns to refrain from taking action until it receives permission to do so from someone else. Over time, you become wary and begin to harbor misgivings about your ability to perform.

Recognize that you possess a unique value. Your knowledge, skills, talents, and adaptability eliminate the need for external validation. As long as your confidence levels are aligned with reality, you can be self-assured and self-assertive when you face uncertainty.

Self-confidence is one of the keystones to mental toughness. It's difficult to develop the latter without first possessing the former. Fortunately, changing how you see yourself is relatively simple because it's based on recognizing your existing value. Adjusting your self-perception is steeped in actuality rather than the unkind phantoms that result from your inner critic's condemnation.

EXERCISE

Create a shortlist of things that regularly hurt your confidence. This might include negative self-talk, a messy workspace, a sloppy physical appearance, or an absence of personal boundaries. Everyone is different, and therefore your list will be unique to you.

Next, write down actions you can take to reduce the effect of each item on your self-confidence. Be specific. For example, if you struggle with negative self-talk, you might commit to confronting your inner critic whenever it speaks. If it claims, "You're going to fail," you might respond with, "You're wrong, and here's why."

Finally, address one item a time. Take the actions you listed to lessen the item's impact on your confidence levels. Repetition and consistency are your allies in this exercise.

The time required: 20 minutes.

How Your Attitude Affects Your Mental Toughness

Our attitude heavily influences our behavior. It sets the tone for how we approach difficult situations and respond to them. It largely dictates our psychological resilience when we encounter adversity, and determines the actions we take to overcome - or surrender to - it.

If we have a positive attitude, we're likely to evaluate situations with optimism and confidence. If we have a negative attitude, we're likely to evaluate them with cynicism and fear. Our behavioral responses to setbacks, challenges, and obstacles will spring from these feelings.

Overcoming Your Circumstances vs. Expecting Them to Change

When someone tells us to "stay positive," we immediately think of the stereotypical positive thinker who goes through life, expecting everything to turn out fine. This individual seems to be oblivious to their circumstances. He ignores life's difficulties, confident they'll simply disappear of their own accord. He experiences no emotional distress because he expects life's misfortunes to sort them out.

In short, the stereotypical positive thinker presumes his circumstances will change to suit him. If life were a journey, he sees himself as a mere passenger with little to no influence on the events happening around him.

But this image is mistaken

Keeping a positive attitude isn't about harboring baseless optimism. It's not about having faith that things will simply work themselves out. It's about recognizing that we can positively influence our circumstances, prevailing over misfortune and hardship under our talents, abilities, and capacity to adapt.

This positive outlook, which importance stems from self-confidence, is a requisite partner to our mental toughness. It dictates how we feel when we encounter complications. It governs how we respond to them. This mindset spurs us to assert ourselves, taking purposeful action rather than remaining passive and hoping for the best.

The Importance of Commitment

When we commit to something, we assign value to it. The outcome we seek becomes, in our estimation, worthy of the time and effort required to pursue it. Our actions and decisions become focused on making it a reality. Our commitment not only encourages us to exert effort toward achieving our desired outcome but also coaxes us to persist when things fail to go our way.

For example, suppose you start a side business. You commit to making it a success. This commitment encourages you to spend time on it during the evenings and weekends. But it does more than that.

If you've ever run a business, even a small one from a corner of your bedroom, you know a myriad of things can go wrong. And sometimes, they do so suddenly and without warning. Lacking commitment, you might be tempted to throw your hands in the air and say, "I give up!" Instead, your pledge to make your business a success prompts you to roll up your sleeves and work to overcome whatever roadblocks you've encountered.

Committing to a task, project, or specific outcome gives us the resilience to stay positive and resolute when we face obstacles. Our commitment helps us to endure when giving up would be easier. It allows us to persist, working toward our goals rather than surrendering them for short-term gratification.

The Willingness to Pursue Continuous Growth

As noted above, a positive attitude gives us confidence that we can overcome adversity. This frame of mind is reinforced whenever we learn new skills (or improve existing ones), absorb new information, or encounter new situations. Our competence and proficiency increases, and with it, our self-assuredness.

For this reason, we must pursue growth in all matters related to our commitments. Pursuing growth in matters that extend *beyond* our commitments is beneficial. Doing so exposes us to unfamiliar situations, which allow us to expand our skill set and knowledge base.

Mentally tough people have a growth mindset. They believe their abilities are not set in stone. Rather, they trust they can learn *new* abilities, often by persevering when life becomes difficult. These individuals are rarely inclined to give up. They perceive their shortcomings as areas that warrant improvement and setbacks as opportunities to learn from their mistakes.

A growth mindset is integral to cognitive resilience. It's an essential component of a positive attitude. The underlying belief that we can constantly improve ourselves, and thereby achieve things that were impossible for us in the past is essential to becoming mentally strong. It reinforces our self-confidence, which amplifies our willingness to stay the course when we encounter adversity.

There's one last element that directly impacts our attitude and, with it, our capacity for resilience: gratitude.

The Art of Being Grateful

Many people wallow in self-pity. They grumble about how life is unfair and why their circumstances prevent them from accomplishing their goals. These folks are preoccupied with their own unhappiness. They indulge in victimhood rather than acknowledging their talents and abilities. This frame of mind leads to perpetual frustration and can even open the door to depression.

Unsurprisingly, people who habitually feel sorry for themselves often give up when they're confronted by challenges.

It's important to recognize that self-pity is a choice. It's an attitude we adopt rather than one that overtakes us. Once we adopt this negative attitude, it can quickly gain a foothold in our minds, prompting us to blame our failures on our circumstances instinctively. This frame of mind is contrary to developing mental toughness.

When we express gratitude, we underscore the fact.

Chapter 17
Improve Your Attitude

If you want to be truly successful in life, you should start doing rather than merely thinking. The first task you need to do is adopt a positive attitude. Once your heart is filled with the light of optimism and enthusiasm, you will see a dramatic rise in the opportunities you have and a significant fall in the number of problems in your life. Positivity is essential for people who love to lead others. Only a person who has a positive attitude can compel other people to take a specific action.

The Reasons to Change Your Mindset

Have you ever wondered what impact changing your mindset can have on your success and failure? What we believe can significantly affect what we achieve in life. What is the mindset? A mindset generally alludes to qualities such as your talent and the stock of intelligence you have. Some people have a fixed mindset, and they believe that some qualities are inborn, and they cannot be changed while others have a growth mindset, who believes that everyone can develop individual abilities through hard work and commitment. This notion can be explained by a simple example. Some children view every problem as a challenge that they must solve. They try to find something to learn from the experience. Other students view complex problems as impossible to solve. They get depressed thinking that their intelligence is being judged and scrutinized. The children who view challenges in a positive light have growth mindsets while the second group of children has fixed mindsets.

Our mindset plays a crucial role in shaping our personality and helps us cope with the daily challenges of life. If a student has a growth mindset, he or she will be able to bring about significant changes in their life when it comes to making an effort in job hunting or starting a new business. Also, people who have a growth mindset exhibit a higher level of resilience in the wake of failures. A growth mindset enables them to show perseverance when they are subjected to setbacks. On the contrary, people with fixed mindsets tend to give up easily.

One particularly bad habit of people with fixed mindsets is that they always need approval from others. They live to please others, and that's why their biggest fear is rejection from society. They care a lot about how society will react to whatever they do. Will they be perceived as a winner or a loser? These thoughts play a significant role in putting a halt to their growth. On the contrary, people with growth mindsets have a hunger for learning. They believe that every experience they have is teaching them a valuable lesson. They also love challenges because they teach them something new.

Factors at Play on Forming a Mindset

Generally, people across the world have two types of mindsets that are constructed by their experiences at home or school. Let's explore how these two types come into existence.

- A child will have a fixed mindset if he or she is taught that he or she should look smart rather than seek learning. This leads them to focus on how other people are judging them. They are always fearful that they may not be able to live up to the expectations of those around them.

- A child will have a growth mindset if he or she is taught not to see mistakes as setbacks. They are encouraged by parents and teachers to try new things. They also learn from their mistakes and see this as an opportunity to build on their potential.

A growth mindset doesn't mean that a child starts thinking that he or she can conquer the world just as Einstein and Newton did. Instead, it means that he or she learns to live up to the maximum potential their life has to offer.

You can tell the type of mindset you have by studying your personality traits. For example, some people naturally are more intelligent than others. People are unable to change their necessary abilities and personality traits. Some people think that talent cannot be acquired and what they naturally have cannot be changed. If you have thoughts like these, you have a fixed mindset.

On the other hand, some people have the power to change themselves. They believe that they can learn new things, and their intelligence has the capacity to grow and improve. Also, they are not shy of working hard and acquiring and practicing new skills for the development of latent abilities. If you can think like this, you have a growth mindset.

Why Change Your Mindset?

Change is constant, and it influences every decision we make and the path we take in our lives. Things are changing around us at a fast pace, and we have to keep up to succeed in life. The business landscape is changing fast, and new industries are jumping in. Technology is taking the world by storm by making its way into different fields. Change is an ideal path to happiness and success. I believe that our minds are potent gadgets, and by changing them, we can change the course of our lives. We can improve our lives if we can change the way we think and react to different experiences and thoughts. Our happiness depends on who we are and who we want to be. Here is a breakdown of the signs that indicate that you should change your mindset.

1. If you are continually focusing on the wrong thing, you need to change your mindset. Sometimes, your mind fixates itself on disappointments and worries, and it just fails to see the positivity that comes your way. I don't say bad things don't exist, or they don't affect you at all, but there are high chances that a few aspects of your life remain in good shape. All you need to do is be thankful for the good things in your life because it will help keep the bad things out of your path. If you make it a habit of ignoring the good things in your life, there is a higher chance that you will not be able to use them to your advantage.

2. You are in desperate need of changing your mindset if you happen to find yourself angry about suffering from a loss, and you don't believe in celebrating your victories. You always think that failure

lurks behind each victory you have, and that's why you cannot be grateful for life's precious moments, even when you are succeeding. You cannot appreciate what you have achieved, and this leads to frustration and dejection. This indicates a negative mindset, and you need to change it. You need to realize that if you keep casting doubts on your victories, you will remain ungrateful for what you have achieved.

3. A time may come in your life when you stop facing the truth. For example, the sky is overcast with clouds, and it is raining on end for two days. You can curse all you want in the clouds and rain, but this won't make the sun come out. Complaints agitate your brain but do nothing else to change the situation. If you are not earning enough, you can change this by working harder; but there are some things that you simply cannot change, such as the weather. You need to start accepting reality as it is to bring about a change in your mindset.

4. You need to change your mindset if you are always complaining about what you have in life versus what you don't have. Being ambitious is what everyone should strive for, but too much of it blinds us to all the blessings in our lives that we already have. For example, if you want a luxurious bungalow your friend owns and a sports car he drives while you live in a contemporary house and drive a Prius, you should not forget the time when you lived in a log house, and you used to travel by bus. Striving for the best is something everyone wishes for, but sometimes this lands us in a

situation where we are never satisfied with what we have. This creates a vacuum that just cannot be filled.

5. If you like to play the victim role, your mindset needs a change. I am not saying that you have never been wronged by people. There may come a time when you have been victimized by those close to you in some unfavorable circumstances. When you feel that you have been victimized, you should ask this one question to yourself: Does victimize myself empower me? Be honest with yourself. Even if you have been victimized before, rejecting that role will help you take up a new and more decisive role. Something that can surely empower you more.

6. People always welcome dramatic endings and emotional scenes into their minds willingly. They welcome them so much that they go on to create some themselves at times. It has been evident over the past few years through research that people who have negative mindsets give space to alien thoughts that should not belong in their minds. These thoughts include messages from your parents, convincing you that you are a failure and that you cannot pursue your dreams. The thoughts can be messages from your intimate partner who diminishes your worth as a romantic partner. You should immediately eliminate these scenarios and thoughts from your mind if you want to change your mindset. These thoughts are not yours. They are based on the thoughts of other people and reflect their judgments. Let go of them and clear your mind.

7. Disagreements are a normal part of human interaction from time to time. However, if you happen to be regularly disagreeing with people, it may indicate that you need a change of mindset. I am not talking about the people whom you meet on the street; I am talking about the people whom you trust and whom you respect in your life.

8. We don't always get what we want in life. This is just how the world operates. Your expectations remain unfulfilled sometimes, and healthy people realize this fact, but if you get angry and frustrated about unfulfilled expectations, you are not on the right track. If all your expectations are getting fulfilled, it is unnatural and unearthly. Expectations have a significant impact on our minds. If we continually set high expectations, we will never be satisfied with our lives, and this will lead to frustration and annoyance. For example, say you set a goal to be a billionaire by 45 but are nowhere near to reaching that goal. There is no doubt that you will feel frustrated. Some people are gifted with exceptional skills, and they achieve this goal even before the target age they set, but not everyone can be like Elon Musk, the CEO of Tesla, who achieved everything so early in his life. Instead of building unrealistic expectations and increasing internal pressure, you should tune your mindset to think realistically and thrive in this world.

Change Your Vision

A person's mission statement is a personal constitution for them that becomes the foundation for making life-changing decisions. It allows a person to adapt to changes in their life. If you want to succeed in life, you must create a personal mission statement to pursue, but it is also a fact that you cannot just write it overnight. It takes time. You have to answer several questions that come into your mind, such as the 'why' factor in your life.

Chapter 18
The Purpose of your Life

Recognize that discovering the objective of one's life is a tortuous course, comprised of failings and also caring frustrations, yet it is a course that deserves requiring completion. The method in which we respond to the challenges of our life assists us in recognizing that we are, and also, despite everything we do not proceed as well as quit on that particular method, we understand that it is the appropriate one for us. Locating our objective is a trip that can last a lifetime, or our objective is clear to us quickly, nevertheless our demands transform as we transform throughout the years

Your life function contains the primary inspiring purposes of your life-- the factors you stand up in the early morning.

The objective can assist life choices, affect actions, form objectives, use a feeling of instructions, and also produce significance. Some individuals might discover their objective plainly revealed in all these facets of life.

The objective will certainly be unique for everybody; what you determine as your course might be various from others. What's even more, your function can transform as well as move throughout life in reaction to the progressing top priorities as well as variations of your very own experiences.

The definition of life is to provide life significance.

Ken Hudgins

It's fascinating. I obtain a varied blend of exactly how they recognize what a life objective is when I chat to close friends as well as associates regarding the objective. Some understand their function without effort; others never ever also asked themselves the concern.

What Does Life Purpose Mean?

Function implies the factor for the presence. Simple and also ordinary.

Life function is the factor for your presence. Tweet this!

When you're addressing the concern of your life's objective, you are addressing: Why do you exist?

And also, you need to determine your means as well as proactively provide a solution to that concern. As the quote from Ken Hudgins recommends: The objective of life is to live life purposefully. And also this is entirely approximately you.

The Objective is Direction

Why would certainly it make feeling to specify your objective?

Recognizing your function will certainly offer you clear instructions in life. If you recognize your life function, you will undoubtedly get quality and also have the advantage of an internal assisting system. As well as following this course will undoubtedly accomplish you with implying in life. A significance that you establish on your own.

Your life objective resembles the best objective you have in your life. It's your vision for just how you want your life will undoubtedly be.

In The 7 Habits, Stephen Covey pointed out an intriguing workout where you would undoubtedly compose the speech at your very own funeral service. This is disclosing exactly how you want to see your life end up inevitably.

Outer as well as Internal Purpose

It was Eckhart Tolle that claimed that there is genuinely 2 types of functions:

The very first is continuing to meet your internal objective, which is to expand knowingly within. The external objective is what you lay out to attain on your own in life. While you go after it, you have to do it knowingly, in many other words: live currently in every minute.

If I look at my experiences with living and also adhering to the objectives in the existing minute, this makes a great deal of feeling. You need to make room and also not shed on your own exclusively in your external function. It would undoubtedly be a catch.

The mix of an effective job, a caring household, as well as a solid social media network, might appear like the dish for the best life. Also, those that can inspect each of those boxes may feel like something is missing out on-- and also that "something" is their function in life.

"Finding your function" is greater than simply a saying or a desire that will certainly never be met. It's a device for a much better, better, much healthier life that also a couple of individuals try to use.

Just around 25 percent of American grown-ups mention having a clear feeling of function regarding what makes their lives significant.

Why Do You Need a Sense of Purpose?

A 2010 research study released in Applied Psychology discovered that people with high degrees of eudemonic wellness-- which includes having a feeling of objective together with a feeling of control as well as sensation like what you do is worthwhile-- often tend to live longer. Scientists located that individuals with the best wellness were 30 percent much less most likely to pass away throughout the eight-and-a-half-year follow-up duration.

There's likewise study that connects sensation as if you have a feeling of function to favorable health and wellness results, such as fewer strokes and also cardiovascular disease, much better rest as well as a reduced danger of mental deterioration and also specials needs.

A 2016 research study released in the Journal of Research, as well as Personality, discovered that people that feel a feeling of function make even more cash than people that feel as though their job does not have a definition.

The excellent information is, you do not have to pick in between having a wide range as well as living a purposeful life. You could locate the even more objective you have, the even more cash you'll make.

With every one of those advantages, it's clear that it's essential to locate objects as well as significance in your life. It's not something that can be identified promptly.

The procedure calls for a lot of self-reflection, paying attention to others as well as locating where your interests exist.

Currently, just how do you locate your objective is life, just how do you uncover your function.

Tips to assist you in discovering your life enthusiasm as well as real objects.

1. Check out the important things You Love to Do & What Comes Easy to You

We are all birthed with a purposeful as well as a deep objective that we have to find. You can start to uncover your enthusiasm or your objective of discovering 2 points:

- What do you like to do?

- What comes conveniently to you?

Obviously, it takes a job to create your skills- also one of the most talented artists still needs to practice-but it ought to feel all-natural, like rowing downstream as opposed to upstream. I like to instruct, to compose, to trainer, to assist in, to educate, and also to create transformational workshops, workshops, as well as programs. I enjoy bringing various other leaders with each other for seminars and also to co-create brand-new techniques to our job.

I spent lots of years in finding out exactly how to understand these abilities. I enjoyed every minute of it. If you are enduring as well as having a hard time, you are most likely not living on an objective.

2. Ask Yourself What Qualities You Enjoy expressing one of the most worldwide

Ask for your own, what are two higher qualities I most take pleasure in revealing in the globe? Mine is love and also happiness.

Second, ask for your own, what are two means I most appreciate sharing these top qualities? Mine is motivating as well as encouraging individuals. I motivate individuals with the relocating tales that I inform in my workshops, which I blog about in my publications, and also, I equip them by showing them effective success techniques that they can use in their very own lives.

3. Produce a Life Purpose Statement

If it were running flawlessly according to you, take a couple of minutes as well as create a summary of what the globe would certainly look like. In my best globe, everyone is living their greatest vision where they are doing, being, as well as having whatever they desire. Integrate all three right into one declaration, as well as you will certainly have a clear concept of your function. Mine is "Inspiring and also encouraging individuals to live their highest possible vision in a context of love as well as happiness."

4. Follow Your Inner Guidance (What Is Your Heart Telling You?).

Suppose I informed you that you have your very own support system within you that can aid you receive from where you remain in life to where you wish to go?

It's called your internal GPS. Your internal GPS resembles the GPS system you make use of in your vehicle or on your phone. It informs you exactly how to receive from factor A to factor B.

When you enter your auto as well as are heading to a detailed location, what is the first thing you input right into your GPS? It discovers your existing place. It offers you instructions to where you are heading once it's figured out where you are.

For the system to function, it merely requires to recognize your start place and also your end location. The navigating system determines the remainder by the use of an onboard computer system that obtains signals from numerous satellites as well as determines your precise setting. It stories an excellent training course for you. All you need to do from that factor is to comply with the guidelines it provides you to reach your location.

Choose Where You Want to Go

All you need to do is make a decision where you wish to pass clarifying your vision, after that secure your location via personal goal setting, affirmations, as well as visualization, and after that, begin taking the activities that will certainly relocate you in the ideal instructions. With every image you picture, you're "inputting" the location you intend to reach.

Every single time you reveal a choice for something, you are revealing an intent.

A table by the home window, front row seats at a seminar, superior tickets, a space with sea sight, or a caring partnership.

All these ideas, as well as pictures, are sending out demands to deep space.

If you avoid of its means-- indicating you do not disrupt the procedure with a stream of adverse ideas questions, as well as anxieties, your internal GPS will certainly maintain unraveling the following steps along your path as you remain to progress.

To put it simply, as soon as you clear up and after that, remain concentrated on your vision (you can do this with a vision board or reflection), the specific actions will certainly maintain showing up along the road in the form of inner support, developing suggestions, and also brand-new chances.

5. Be Clear About Your Life Purpose.

When you are clear concerning what you desire as well as maintain your mind frequently concentrated on it, the just how will certainly maintain turning up.

When you are on or off training course by the quantity of happiness you are experiencing, you were birthed with internal assistance that informs you. The important things that bring you the best delight remain in positioning with your function and also will certainly obtain you to where you intend to go.

You will certainly be shocked as well as impressed by what it supplies when you offer your objectives to the cosmos with all its effective innovation. This is where the magic, as well as wonders, occur. Take a while to believe truthfully as well as honestly concerning where you presently remain in your life and also what you intend to finish with your life.

Exactly how are your connections going? As well as so on.

Conclusion

We all experience successes and failures in the course of normal creative activity; they are natural indicators of results. However, the idea of failure can get out of control and become a complete mentality that begins to feed and continue in a way that creates restrictive conditions for our conscience and excludes many of the unlimited possibilities that are a natural consequence of our creative power. Can we do something about it if we discover that we are influenced by such thinking? Or will it continue to stop us and tear us down forever to deny us the creative success that is our birthright?

The failure of thought is generally established in our early years due to social and physical environmental influences. In some cases, however, this can be determined by a series of unusual negative events for which we are not prepared by force and character. A short article does not allow an exhaustive study of the origins of wrong thinking, but I will provide a link to a good resource at the end of this article. Instead, it is much more important to take a look at how the error mentality looks and how it works, and possibly ways to counteract it.

We are what we believe

If we reduce success and failure to its simplest basis, we can say: "If we believe we are successful, we will succeed, and if we believe we are failures, we will be failures." While this is the case, there is no indication of the challenges we face or how we have to face them. The most powerful concept to consider here is conditioning. Virtually all of our thought and behavior patterns are created through this powerful behavior change technique. And its strength lies in its simplicity. What we are repeatedly exposed to overtime becomes a habitual pattern in us.

The failure mentality is generated and maintained by the negative limiting thinking patterns that we have been allowed to establish in our subconscious mind and consciousness, and once we accept it, we become the administrators of these depressed and negatively failed thinking habits of This way, we help ourselves. Perpetuate The fact that we have allowed them to exist and keep them up to date with the thoughts of our own mind is proof that we have the creative power to do something about these thought patterns.

Tools and equipment

The task of replacing negative thinking and long-established behavior patterns with new, positive, and bright constructive ones is like a trip, and this trip may require that we make short mini-trips along the way. Do not fret. You can do it, many others have successfully followed this path, and so have you. However, you need some tools and equipment that will not only help you get there, but also help you overcome occasional bumps. Meditation will be your Swiss army knife and the most important tool. Well, do not raise your hands desperate for that. A lot of people have not thought about how useful this tool can be. But you must overcome all the traditional images of the monks in the Himalayas and start thinking about saws, hammers, and levels.

There will be difficult times on the road to our goals and dreams. These difficult times are due to situations and problems in our families, businesses, professions, and in our own private life. The secret to the success of your leadership in these difficult situations is that you are strong and brave in this process.

"I am not talking about physical strength. I am talking about mental and emotional strength." If a leader fails, he must be strong. When a leader is emotionally exhausted, he has to be strong. If a leader is disappointed, he must be strong. If a leader develops an action plan to succeed, and his plan is interrupted by unexpected circumstances, he must be strong.

A great leader knows that life on the road to success and greatness will have difficult times. With this awareness, he/she needs to be mentally prepared beforehand to deal effectively with adversity and distractions.

If we develop our talents and leadership talents, we can anticipate more problems and solutions, anticipate the chances of success, and discover the unique qualities that hide in us.

Self-education and leadership development allows a great leader to develop a quiet and peaceful fortress. "This development will create the leadership attribute of trust and calm even in the most difficult situations." I know that it is easier said than done in some of these situations to be calm and safe. Some situations in life can make you throw a curveball so fast that you cannot see it. "But if you want to be great and realize your vision, calm and trust are a necessity. They work together effectively, hand in hand." You should not think in a limited way about these situations, always think BIG. "When you think big, the mentality of a winner arises.

Key point: while working on your goals, some of your plans may not work as you expect. Ask many executives who received their pink notes this week. In your delicate situation, you MUST be strong and be ready to make "adjustments" to your action plan. Keep your eyes wide open and concentrate on the dream and vision you want for your life. Imagine the final result while adjusting your plan. "This mental image of your success is your daily inspiration. Your daily inspiration makes you a champion, and the champions overcome difficult times."

What is your attitude right now? Do you observe your future as a glass half empty or half full? Is your opinion a portal of what you want from your company or a reminder of what you have not achieved? The year 2009 was brutal for many small business owners and a real challenge for almost everyone who has to work their way in business. And although we all tend to depend on the most tangible resources to build businesses; Money, time, experience, plans, and support, to name a few, our greatest asset is our ability to control our minds.

Your mentality influences your thinking, your perceptions, your beliefs, and your behavior. It is the little voice in the back of your mind that has an opinion about everything you do or want to do that determines how you think about your current situation. As a small business consultant, I often encounter small business owners who question their ability to progress and discover how to do business in a market where all the rules of the game have been voided.

The reality is we have a difficult economic situation. Many companies will not survive this long belt adjustment because they could not see a successful result. It is hard to see other entrepreneurs disappear, especially if they saw robust growth a few years ago. The fact is that some companies survive and strengthen even more once the market returns. Are you still a dominant player in 2010?

I am currently seeing the biggest loser. There are some incredible achievements of people who have been so degraded that they have lost all hope. What individual has in common is that they strive and learn to improve their mental and physical situations. They were given the support and responsibility to maintain the course until the results arrived. They believed in what they could not see once. The same transformation can happen for business owners, and the clients of my business coaching program enjoy daily.

Creativity

Although creative power is something natural for the human species, it is not fully developed as a piece of standard equipment. We have become a mentally vague species, and it is not difficult to understand why. Our minds and brains are not the easiest landscape to explore, especially because it requires self-confidence and self-discipline to develop, two of the least popular goals everyone has on their list. But if we want to make changes in our lives, we have to bite the ball and endure hard work.

It is unlikely that the development of self-confidence and self-discipline will take epidemic proportions in the current superficial civilization, where the satisfaction of selfish youthful desires is the main driving force and agenda. This will make it difficult to achieve our goals, and there will not be a long list of people to help you with your efforts and to help you. So get ready for a hard and often lonely trip. The development of the characteristics of self-confidence and self-discipline is part of the greater development of our greatest capacity, which is our unlimited creative power, and some tools will help us get there.

10% of the sale of this book is destined for the Fundación Letras Itinerantes, dedicated to promoting reading in Mayan communities, preserving the language and providing quality education in Quintana Roo, Mexico.

CPSIA information can be obtained
at www.ICGtesting.com
Printed in the USA
LVHW022344140121
676462LV00003B/354

9 781801 098717